MEN MET ALONG THE TRAIL

Adventures in Archaeology

MEN MET ALONG THE TRAIL

Adventures in Archaeology

BY
NEIL M. JUDD

UNIVERSITY OF OKLAHOMA PRESS

NORMAN

BY NEIL M. JUDD

The Bureau of American Ethnology: A Partial History
Men Met Along the Trail: Adventures in Archaeology
(Norman, 1968)

LIBRARY OF CONGRESS CATALOG CARD NUMBER: 68–10300

PREFACE

THESE REMINISCENCES of fifty years' work were suggested by four younger associates with the thought that some of my experiences might prove amusing as well as instructive. They are the experiences of a student archaeologist who has seen our discipline evolve from curio-collecting to radiocarbon-dating and pollen analysis.

The illustrations, unless otherwise identified, are from negatives by the author and have all been given to the various public archives.

NEIL M. JUDD

Silver Spring, Maryland
September 16, 1968

CONTENTS

vii

ILLUSTRATIONS

ix

MEN MET ALONG THE TRAIL

Adventures in Archaeology

I

NINETEEN HUNDRED AND SEVEN

PROFESSOR BYRON CUMMINGS was one of the most influential men in my life. I was a student in his Greek and Latin classes at the University of Utah in 1907 when he invited me to accompany him on an exploring expedition to White Canyon in San Juan County. The year before—in 1906—he had learned of prehistoric ruins in widely scattered sections of the state. Since no one else seemed interested, he inaugurated classes in Utah archaeology, started the University Museum singlehandedly, and did all the cataloging and caretaking himself. Each summer he raised the money for annual field work and personally met the usual deficit. This I know because I was his volunteer assistant from 1907 through 1909.

On the trail with him those three years, I developed a genuine admiration for Professor Cummings. A deeply religious man, he found reward wherever the trail led. He saw the hand of the Creator on every mountain, shrub, and wind-worn rock. He was the only Caucasian I ever knew, other than Professor Herbert E. Gregory of Yale, who could outwalk a horse in desert sand.

There were a few who did not like Byron Cummings. He had a mind of his own and was not easily bent to another's point of view. His many sterling qualities were rooted in a background of privation and sacrifice of which he never spoke. Born in Westville, New York, on September 20, 1860, the youngest son of a Union soldier who did not survive the

3

Civil War, he was graduated from Rutgers in 1889, and he taught at the University of Utah from 1893 to 1915.

In 1915 he was invited to the University of Arizona to become professor of archaeology and director of the State Museum; he held both positions until his retirement twenty-three years later. During his tenure at Arizona he was twice designated acting president, in 1921 and 1927. Former students remember him as the faculty member who remained on duty, day and night, during the flu epidemic of 1918. Having served two universities as dean of arts and sciences, Professor Cummings was affectionately known on both campuses as "the Dean," and that is the way I knew him.

The party which Dean Cummings assembled in 1907 for exploration of White Canyon in southeastern Utah included two student archaeologists—of whom I was one—two engineering students as surveyors, a journalist, and a minister. Edgar L. Hewett, director of the School of American Research and representing The Archaeological Institute of America, the parent organization through which the Utah society had obtained its permit, was present for a few days in his usual supervisory capacity. Dean Cummings himself did most of the fuel-gathering, water-toting, and cooking. He attended to the camp drudgery because he assumed that any adult should know when help was needed. He never gave orders. Since he was a master of the Dutch oven and frying pan, it was easier for him to prepare a meal for all than to coach the less willing or the less efficient.

The frying pan and the coffeepot were indispensable, but the cast-iron Dutch oven was the most versatile utensil in the chuck wagons of the West. With hot coals above and below, a well-seasoned Dutch oven was capable of producing an unparalleled batch of baking-powder biscuits and then the gravy to go with them. In capable hands it could bake a cake, pie, or pudding. Buried in campfire ashes overnight, it supplied a steaming plate of baked beans for breakfast.

In those faraway days flour came in twenty-five-pound cotton sacks; Arbuckle's coffee, in one-pound paper bags. Those who wanted coffee for breakfast soon learned to crush the roasted beans between a couple of rocks, either in an empty sack or in a blanket. The less fastidious made biscuits by rolling back the top of the flour sack, stirring in the necessary amount of salt, baking powder, bacon grease, and water, and transferring gobs of dough to the preheated oven.

Bluff City, on the north bank of the San Juan River, was the initial destination of the 1907 party. At Thompson's Spring, a way stop on the Denver and Rio Grande Western, we were met by Munroe Redd and his four-horse team from Monticello. Thompson's Spring did not amount to much at that time—a low, faded-red station with a telegraph operator as traffic controller, a near-by coal chute and water tank to replenish engines after the long upgrade from Grand Junction, and that was all. From Thompson's by four-horse wagon it was a day and a half or two days to Moab and then two more days to Monticello; from Monticello, if one wanted to complete the trip by wagon, it was another two days to Bluff. Twenty-five or thirty miles was a day-long drive.

Leaving Thompson's Spring in the early morning, a member of our party asked the station agent if he might use the urinal. "Urinal! My god, man," shrieked the agent as he swept the room with an open palm. "Right outside that door is 40,000 acres and not a tree on it."

From the railway our road crossed an open valley that seemed endlessly long and tedious. There was nothing to do but lounge among the bedrolls and talk, and we soon tired of talking. To right and left brushless, dun-colored clay reached for the horizon. Our plodding horses traveled at a walk and there was plenty of time for exploring, but no one ventured far from the wagon. There were no visible ruins to examine, no mound prominent enough to waken one's curiosity. Not until later did we learn of hieroglyphs and open caves back of Thompson's, of sandstone arches and fantastically carved cliffs a short distance east of the road we followed. We passed no one and no one passed us. Our concern was to get to Moab and its fruit-filled orchards and then on to the summer's program.

By way of the barren flat south of Thompson it was an all-day journey to the old cable ferry across the Grand River just short of Moab. That ferry, its cable slapping the waves as it pulled itself across, operated on a first-come, first-served basis, and one never knew what to expect at the crossing. Sometimes a flock of sheep had precedence, and, with sheep, where one went all wanted to go.

Approximately midway between the railroad and the ferry was "Court House Hotel," a two-room stone structure where the stagecoach changed horses and where one could buy a meal of sorts after chasing off the chickens. It was a picturesque establishment in its prime, but undoubtedly has since succumbed to progress, along with the river and the ferry. In 1921 some person in authority changed the name of the Grand River to "the Colorado," and thirty-four years later a magnificent new bridge replaced the old cable ferry at a cost of $452,000.

Some ten miles beyond Moab we came to Hatch Wash and camped for the night. Nearly everyone who traveled in the area camped at Hatch Wash. A rocky outcrop offered shelter from wind-blown sand, and water was to be had in the arroyo. But there was no forage near by; thus the freighters always carried hay and oats for their horses and fuel for cooking. The choice of camping place went to the first arrival, one spot was as good as another.

It was at Hatch Wash in 1907 that I learned, once and for all, never to spread my bedroll in a roadway. The sun had gone down that night in traditional splendor—a gorgeous display of reds and pinks and purples; the stars had burst from a cloudless sky and were almost within reach. But sometime after our party retired a storm passed overhead, and before I could get out of the way a muddy rivulet came racing down the wheel track right through my bed tarp and blankets. The spot had seemed such a clever selection, with our wagon blocking all traffic and the wheel rut just deep enough and wide enough to hold my canvas-covered bed.

By daybreak, with coyotes still yapping across the valley, our driver had watered his horses and rationed their morning oats. After a breakfast of bacon, baking-powder biscuits, and black coffee our course continued on south, past the forested slopes of the La Sals and then upgrade to Monticello at the foot of the Blue Mountains.

Monticello was home for Munroe Redd and his team, but after a day's rest for replenishing supplies we were off again, first to a charming little glen appropriately named Verdure and then down a long, pine-shaded road to Canyon Diablo. After the Devil's Canyon we crossed the sun-drenched miles of White Mesa and then, finally, passed down a rocky stairway that opened upon the valley of the San Juan River and Bluff City.

Bluff City was Dean Cummings' approach to White Canyon in 1907 as it was his gateway to Oljeto a year later. His chief purpose in 1907 was to prepare a topographic map of White Canyon and to locate thereon its three natural bridges and rumored prehistoric ruins. The three bridges were known

7

locally as the Augusta, the Carolyn, and the Edwin. The Augusta and the Carolyn were so designated in *The Century Magazine* of August, 1904, in an article reporting Utah explorations by Horace J. Long, a mining engineer.

Long had first heard of the White Canyon bridges the year before at Hite, where he had gone for his mail. At Hite he met James A. ("Al") Scorup, a cattleman from Bluff City, and Scorup had agreed to guide him to White Canyon. Placer-mining along the Colorado River was just past its peak, and Cass Hite's camp, on the west side of the river east of the Henry Mountains, was a convenient meeting place for prospectors and engineers. Hite was still a one-man town in 1907, although its post office, if one ever existed, was no longer functioning. Such mail as Cass Hite then received came horseback from Hanksville, fifty miles to the west.

Thus the popular names by which the White Canyon natural bridges were widely known in 1907 originated with that chance 1903 meeting between Long and Scorup. Long named the largest of the three bridges "The Augusta," in tribute to his wife; the second, "The Carolyn," honored the mother of his guide. The third and smallest bridge, "The Edwin," was named later for Colonel Edwin F. Holmes, a prominent Salt Lake City citizen and sponsor of a Commercial Club pictorial expedition in 1905.

The fact is rarely mentioned today, but those same White Canyon bridges had been visited in September, 1883, by Cass Hite and three companions, "Indian Joe," Edward Randolph, and "Scotty" Rose, from their retreat down on the Colorado River. As men will, Hite at once set about naming his discovery and, with commendable respect for political stature, designated the three bridges, in order of decreasing size, "The President," "The Senator," and "The Congressman."

8

At the time of our 1907 visit, Hite lived in a post-and-mud hut on the west side of the river, opposite the mouth of White Canyon. He told Dean Cummings that he had prospected both sides of the Colorado but had found no more than a little placer gold "downstream." Years later, chance visitors to my Washington desk told me that "Old Cass" was operating a ferry on an improvised road from Blanding to Hanksville. This report came as a surprise, for I had seen that country from a distance and knew it as only packhorse country. Still later I learned that Cass Hite had died and was buried a stone's throw from his makeshift home and near the grave of a former soldier, name unknown. Since Major Powell's venturesome ride down the Colorado in 1869, various adventurers had dared the canyon waters, mostly in search of gold. But no man asked another where he came from.

Cass Hite remembered the three natural bridges in White Canyon and remembered them well. The Edwin Bridge, or "The Congressman" as he would have called it, pierces a cliff barrier in upper Armstrong Canyon. Great blocks of sandstone were strewn over the slope below; scattered junipers grew between. As our surveyors measured it the bridge was 108 feet high, 175 feet wide, buttress to buttress, and 10 feet thick. It was 28 feet wide and flat-topped. In 1903, Horace J. Long boasted that he was the first white man to ride a horse across Edwin Bridge, a feat subsequently repeated by many. Six men and a horseman stand upon it in one of my 1907 snapshots. One of Dean Cummings' illustrations in the *National Geographic* for February, 1910, shows seventeen horses and riders, men and women, spanning the summit.[1]

Across an intervening gorge, occupying a shallow cave in a jutting rock peninsula, there was a very unusual cliff house,

[1] Vol. XXI, No. 2.

walled and roofed with stone-ax-cut logs, both piñon and juniper. The logs, unnotched at the ends, were piled one upon another; inside, vertical willows held the logs in place; interstices were packed with mud and sandstone spalls. A slab-sided fireplace stood at one end of the main room; in the ceiling there was an obvious hatchway. Providing access from a lower ledge was a very splintery pole, perhaps a later improvisation, but the log-walled dwelling was unquestionably prehistoric, the only one of its kind I have ever seen.

Two or three miles down canyon, past a vast cliffside scribbled with hieroglyphs, we came to the second bridge, the Carolyn, or "The Kachina" as the Park Service would have it. It was a massive structure 186 feet wide by 205 feet in over-all height, squatting across White Canyon at its junction with Armstrong. Several neat little rooms or storage places, some with ceiling timbers and willows still present, graced neighboring ledges and, with them, huge sandstone blocks grooved by the patient rubbing back and forth of stone axes.

What really left a lasting impression at that one-night camp under Carolyn Bridge was my unexpected encounter with a mountain lion. The animal had come to drink at a trail-side pool and, presumably with romance in mind, failed to note my presence. However, just as I was drawing a bucket of water from a deep crevice in the canyon floor, that cougar let go with one of the blood-curdling screams for which its kind is noted—the most god-awful, spine-chilling scream ever heard by human ears. I broke the world's high-jump record right there. The lion left the scene unceremoniously and so did I. Next morning we saw fresh cougar tracks on moist sand both above and downstream from our camp.

Joe Driggs was my companion in searching for ancient ruins. Fred Scranton and J. C. Brown were charged with

10

surveying and mapping the canyon.[2] Lacking Scranton's map, Driggs and I estimated distances between ruins by walking time. This is a poor way to report an archaeological reconnaissance, but it is all I noted at the time and it is all I have today.

The Augusta Bridge, largest and most graceful of the three, spans White Canyon two or three miles above the Carolyn. Our surveyors measured its width, buttress to buttress, as 261 feet; its height from streambed as 222 feet. There were prehistoric habitations both upstream and downstream from the Augusta.

Ruins fifteen minutes below Augusta Bridge: Here at left of the main channel were the remains of a two-part village including at least three kivas. One of these latter had a roof more or less intact and a two-pole ladder protruding through the hatchway and rearward. A second kiva was noteworthy for sizable basal stones on end, and the third, for a single pine log reaching across the middle. To judge from my photographs, these two kivas lacked both bench and pilasters. Here, also, on the lower level and toward the right-hand end of the overhang, were two large chambers, circular and about five and one-half feet deep, their mud-plastered stone walls rounded on top. Each was equipped with a front entrance, oval and deeply rimmed with adobe. There was no evidence of a roof, if any. The angle between the two chambers was occupied by an unplastered stone storage bin, a square hatchway in its flat roof.

On an upper ledge, remains of three or four masonry rooms clung to the rear wall, while out in front of them and close to the cliff edge an intermittent row of stones on end clearly had been placed for defense. Back of and above these re-

[2] *Bulletin of the University of Utah,* Vol. III, No. 3, Pt. 1 (Nov., 1910).

mains, mud-plastered willows slanting up and rearward to the cliff provided household granaries, each having a slanted opening framed by cedar branches and rimmed with adobe.

Ruins ten minutes below Augusta Bridge: Two of my photographs of this narrow ledge-built settlement show doorways: one a ⊤-shaped opening; the second, a fitted sandstone slab in an end wall, probably a storeroom. Above and at the left of this door slab, darker adobe with small in-pressed spalls evidences post-construction repairs.

Village fifteen minutes above Augusta Bridge: Here are remains of a sizable, two-part village for which I find no notes. One part occupies a cave some fifty feet above the valley floor and was apparently entered in ancient times by means of a single pole. A second and smaller timber had been added by visitors sometime prior to 1907, and rundles had been nailed to the two, forming a ladder. To the top of this shorter timber a cottonwood pole had been wired by those same visitors to give aid and comfort over the last twenty feet of smooth sandstone. My lack of notes may, in part, be owing to the fact that the pole slipped a few inches through the wire as I put weight upon it. I got down in a hurry. William Boone Douglass, of the General Land Office, for unknown reasons, named this upper part "The Bear Cave Ruin" during his 1908 survey.

What probably had been the larger portion of this village lay at the base of the fifty-foot cliff, poorly sheltered and now much ruined. To me the most interesting of these lower remains was a pair of storage chambers each made of willows slanted toward the cliff, bound at intervals by horizontal withes and the whole then plastered with mud. My photograph, reproduced by Professor Cummings,[3] shows a fitted

3 *Ibid.,* Vol. III, No. 3, Pt. 2 (Nov., 1910), 23.

sandstone door slab held in place by two cedar wedges which I found in the sand below the door and inserted into split-willow loops on either side. Elsewhere we have read of similar willow loops and of cedar wedges, but here they were found together and they belonged together.

Since this two-part village is the only one I recall in White Canyon that clearly had been plundered in recent years, there are those who will say—and rightfully—that I should have made more notes in passing. Truth is: I didn't know enough. We found these ruins eroded by time but otherwise just as their builders had left them. Our observations were purely superficial. The story that they might have told us has remained for later and better-trained students.

Some of the weird and fantastic rocks along the trail in Armstrong and White canyons, sand-blasted and weather-worn, held a peculiar fascination for me because of their unusual shapes or coloring. But there were other queer rocks and other ruined structures elsewhere: In Coyote Canyon, for instance, and in Grand Gulch. Somewhere in Coyote Canyon we saw a pair of masonry kivas close back under the cliff, one with its roof intact and the other crossed by a single cedar log. In the first of these, both piñon and juniper logs had been utilized in the ceiling and, upon them, a hatchway rimmed with at least four inches of adobe.

Perhaps the most tantalizing ruin of all was a small house cluster in Grand Gulch—a group of rooms high in a small cave guarded by a single wall one stone thick, an upright post for a handhold embedded in the masonry. I inched out along the ledge to grasp the post, but the wall was weak and there was a 500-foot drop below. I was too timid to venture farther.

Near the head of Armstrong Canyon, sheltered by piñons and a detached mass of sandstone but exposed on three sides, were remains of a two-story ruin, the upper-story wall inter-

13

rupted at four-foot intervals by what must have been port-holes. If my fellow archaeologists complain of imprecise location, it should be remembered that the White Canyon area was still unsurveyed in 1907.

Returning to Bluff City after eight weeks in the field without any fresh meat, we had our progress interrupted early one morning when a fat young calf, playfully circling the pack train, fell into a gully and broke its neck. We stopped to have a second breakfast under the nearest tree and wrapped what was left of the carcass in Dean Cummings' bed tarp for transportation to town. The owner of that playful calf expressed his appreciation of our thoughtfulness in bringing home the veal and dismissed the subject. But fifteen years later and nearer the Colorado River, when a fat young calf died under similar circumstances, I noted the brand and reported it, only to be billed for it at Chicago retail prices. To this extent had a recognized custom of the country changed in fifteen short years!

On the near edge of town we met a weather-worn prospector bound for the very region we had recently left. We tried to describe what lay ahead of him but without avail. He showed us his government map on which neither river nor rivulet was indicated north of the San Juan. By that map all was easy walking. When last seen this wanderer was plodding determinedly down the road, his bedroll, shovel, and pan roped to the back of a burro.

Bluff City, on the north bank of the San Juan, was settled in 1879 by Mormon pioneers from west-central Utah. The story of their year-long journey and their conquest of the Colorado River gorge has been told repeatedly, and it should be told again. They were church-ordered to establish a new colony; there was no turning back. Kumen Jones, who drove the first team down through the man-made slit they called

14

"Hole-in-the-Rock," was manager of the community store in the years I knew Bluff City, and a gentler person never lived. The rugged trail up from the Colorado had grown dim, but worn ox shoes and the broken wheels of abandoned wagons provided further reminders of past hardships along the way.

The "Old Swing Tree," under which the original settlers gathered for prayer, succumbed to floods in 1908, but village gardens and green alfalfa fields remained to make Bluff an inviting oasis. Even after half a century I recall with something of nostalgia its sandy streets sheltered by cottonwoods and Lombardy poplars; the warm welcome we found in every pioneer home; the unsung kindnesses of Kumen and Mary Jones, among others; and the bountiful table set by "Aunt Jane" Allen for vigorous young appetites.

Those who never shared a meal prepared by "Aunt Jane" missed an experience not likely to be repeated in this world. Habitually covered by a waist-hung apron, she lived in a two-part log cabin with a dirt roof and a "root cellar" close by the kitchen door. Her pies and cakes were superb and generously portioned; her jams, jellies, pickles, and preserves were heaped upon dishes with flaring rims. The marvel is that her household garden could have produced such a variety of fruits and vegetables and that she had the energy to prepare them. Hers was a labor of self-satisfaction, for there certainly was no profit in what she placed before us students, home from canyon trails.

A short distance upstream from where the "Old Swing Tree" formerly stood were three picturesque formations weathered from the sandstone cliffs and known locally as "The Navaho Twins," "Locomotive Rock," and "The Lone Column," over one hundred feet high. All stood there—and I trust they still stand—evidence of the vagaries of wind,

15

water, and sand. More or less opposite them, on the south side of the river, is a huge crescentic cave with a row of prehistoric dwellings at the back. W. H. Jackson of the Hayden Surveys visited that great cave, high up under the south cliff, on his way to the Hopi Pueblos in 1875. He named the cave "Casa del Eco," in tribute to its remarkable accoustical properties.

Our party was camped under a cottonwood below the mouth of Butler's Wash, its magnificent caves plundered by relic-hunters years before, when a Ute Indian drew rein one day and asked what we were doing. I knew nothing of the Ute language and my knowledge of Navaho was pretty meager, but I managed to convey the idea that we were looking for Anasazis, "the ancient ones," dead people. He knew where to find one and, for a dollar, would show me. So I grabbed a shovel and plodded along behind his horse, up and over one sand dune and then another. That Indian must have ridden a couple of miles around and over drifted sand, looking back frequently and encouraging me with a smile and a cheerful "just a little farther." Finally, when I was becoming a bit weary with this endless pursuit, he stopped outside a wire fence, grinned, and pointed to the Bluff City cemetery. I never trusted another Ute.

With the classroom beckoning and our 1907 season almost at an end, we stopped beside the river trail to examine a three-story ruin. It was here that I first met Alfred V. Kidder, then a Harvard senior. He had arrived at Bluff the night before in a buckboard carrying the weekly mail from Cortez and, being a student of archaeology, had unerringly found his way to our archaeological camp. That chance meeting with Kidder beside the San Juan River was the beginning of a friendship that lasted fifty years. No one has contributed more than he to American prehistory, in the southwestern United

16

States for Peabody Museum of Harvard and the Peabody Foundation for Archaeology, Andover, Massachusetts, and in Middle America for the Carnegie Institution of Washington. Hence it was particularly gratifying when the American Anthropological Association named me 1965 recipient of the Alfred Vincent Kidder Award in recognition of my own contributions to southwestern archaeology, following in Kidder's footsteps.

Professor Cummings' topographic map of White Canyon, prepared by Fred Scranton, was forwarded to E. L. Hewett, representing the Archaeological Institute of America, in Washington and was submitted by him to the General Land Office in the fall of 1907 through Senator Reed Smoot of Utah.[4] Unfortunately, that map is not now to be found, but it undoubtedly prompted President Theodore Roosevelt's proclamation of April 16, 1908, establishing the Natural Bridges National Monument. A month later, on May 15, the General Land Office sent one of its own staff, William Boone Douglass, examiner of surveys, to make a new map. Douglass began his preliminary investigation on June 3; actual surveying continued from September 12 to October 3. Subsequently, on the basis of the Douglass survey, President William Howard Taft issued a second proclamation dated September 25, 1909, superseding that of April 16, 1908, enlarging the area of the Monument and changing the names of its three natural bridges.

At the time of his assignment official instructions charged Mr. Douglass to record the Indian names of the White Canyon bridges, if known. Although the bridges were in Ute territory, the Utes had no names for them either individually or collectively. Therefore, since a United States Geographic

4 Letter of May 23, 1908, from Gifford Pinchot, U.S. Forest Service, to James R. Garfield, Secretary of the Interior.

Board regulation forbids naming any geographic feature after a living person "unless of very great importance and unimpeachable position," three names had to be invented. Douglass in 1909 persuaded the late Walter Hough, then head curator of anthropology at the United States National Museum and a life-long student of the Hopi Indians, to suggest three Indian names. Hough naturally chose Hopi names, basing his choice either on mythology or on local topographic features. These purely fictitious Hopi names have since been substituted for the originals and are firmly fixed in Park Service literature, thus: Sipapu (Augusta), Kachina (Carolyn), and Owachoma (Little or Edwin).

Returning to Monticello at the end of summer, we camped the first night out of Bluff beside a sheepherder's wagon half-hidden among the cedars. A new irrigation ditch guided clean fresh water down from the mountains, and it was that water rather than the wagon and the cedars that urged us into an early camp. We did not know it at the time, but that ditch and wagon marked the future site of Grayson, a name now all but forgotten. Two years after our one-night stop there, red brick buildings stood on every corner and there was talk of a library. Then, according to local tradition, along came a postal inspector named Blanding, who suggested that, in return for a set of U.S. Postal Reports for the library, Grayson change its name to Blanding. And Blanding it has remained ever since, the largest town in San Juan County.

II

NINETEEN HUNDRED AND EIGHT

In 1908, Professor Cummings returned to San Juan County for further explorations. Again he was met at Thompson's Spring, the nearest railroad stop, by Munroe Redd of Monticello—a Mormon and a most estimable gentleman—with his four-horse team and a wagon piled with oats and baled hay. It was an eight-day trip from Monticello to the railroad and back again; for the inevitable dry camp, one wanted feed handy.

Munroe Redd was a farmer; his horses wintered in the home corral and we students spread our bedrolls there, under the sheds. Across the street, a two-story frame house sheltered the family; a roadside ditch brought cool, clear water from the Blue Mountains for both man and beast. We did our own cooking, but Mother Redd, with a knowing estimate of young appetites, occasionally favored us with household delicacies. Her whole-wheat muffins, made from home-ground grain and hot from the oven, were beyond compare.

On one of our infrequent visits to town I saw quiet-voiced Munroe Redd, a rifle balanced on his plow handles, turning the sod for a new field despite threats from the L-C and Carlisle cattle companies whose vast herds roamed the public domain as they had down in New Mexico twenty years before. All this, of course, was prior to the discovery of uranium and the modernization of Monticello.

From Monticello we took saddle horses and pack burros for a brief tour of upper Montezuma Canyon and its tributaries. Traveling this same trail the year before, 1907, Professor Cummings had been halted by Chief Johnny Benow, Posey, and other Ute troublemakers who ordered him to keep going. Not knowing that Scottish and Irish blood flowed through his veins, they tried to frighten the Dean but succeeded only in making him stubborn. He said he would move on next morning and did—on his own schedule—but, meanwhile, he invited two of the visitors to share our supper of stewed tomatoes and baking-powder biscuits.

Those Montezuma Canyon Indians were undoubtedly descendants of the same mixed group—Utes, Navahos, and Piutes—that had stampeded W. H. Jackson's Hayden Surveys pack train in 1875, endangering his photographic record for the entire season; the same outlaw group that had ambushed Gannett and Gardner a few weeks earlier and, about the same time, had run off all the mules and horses of W. H. Holmes's geological party, leaving his men afoot 350 miles from their base in Denver. Thanks to the midnight alertness of Holmes's chief packer, the animals were recovered before daylight, a fact generally unknown today but one that gave name to Recapture Creek, next below the Montezuma.

In later years Jackson saw only amusement in his chance meeting with this wild band of mixed-bloods, even though a careless gesture might have proved tragic. There were only six in his party, including himself; the Indians numbered eighteen or twenty, all young, well mounted, and unafraid. After a brief parley one of them, impatient for action, struck a pack mule with his quirt. Then all set off down canyon, driving the photographic party before them, whooping and hollering, waving quirts and rifles overhead, until they came to a cluster of brush wickiups where their chief graciously invited all to dismount and spend the night.

20

Jackson's thoughts were naturally for his glass plates and cameras, including a 20- by 24-inch monster especially made for the 1875 expedition, while his companions sought to keep their frightened animals from straying. Recalling that noisy, tumultuous escapade in his very readable autobiography (*Time Exposure,* 1940), Jackson remarked: "All of us were having the time of our lives—but in different ways."

The problem of 20- by 24-inch photographs, or even the more common 8 by 10's and 11 by 14's, has greater meaning today if one remembers that Jackson's 1875 negatives were individual pictures each made on a glass plate especially emulsified in a portable darkroom, immediately exposed and immediately developed. Glass, chemicals, and even water had to be transported on muleback. Despite these handicaps, many of Jackson's Rocky Mountain photographs by the old "wet plate" process have never been surpassed.

The Hayden Surveys had been disbanded long before my time, but I heard those 1875 adventures described at firsthand after I moved to Washington in 1911. Holmes, as head curator of the Department of Anthropology, was my first boss in the United States National Museum; Jackson, although a frequent visitor to the capital city, preferred to live in New York, and died there on June 30, 1942, at the age of ninety-nine, refusing to the very last to wear his hearing aid anywhere except in the seclusion of his hotel room. Both were wonderful men, schooled in frontier ways and in city ways, but their individual contributions to the world of art and letters are today unknown to all but a few.

During the course of his 1908 reconnaissance of Upper Montezuma Canyon, Dean Cummings selected for partial examination a large Pueblo III ruin located on the crest of Alkali Ridge some twenty miles south of Monticello and a mile more or less from the spring where camp was estab-

21

lished. Distances along cattle trails can be no more than approximations for the inexperienced, but I will concede nothing from that estimated mile between camp and ruin. We walked to work in the morning and we walked back again at night!

It was Professor Cummings' expedition; he had raised the money to cover field expenses.[1] But E. L. Hewett, still director of the School of American Research, exercising supervisory control over the season's program, came by for a day and named A. V. Kidder, newly graduated from Harvard, to joint command and to be in charge of excavations. Kidder and Cummings were at the ruin every day, but it was Kidder who wrote the report on excavations,[2] and Dean Cummings was left with the chore of cooking (a self-imposed task which he assumed in order to reduce costs).

Hewett had brought with him from Santa Fe his chief photographer, Jesse L. Nusbaum, a tall, blue-faced individual who rode with a case of glass plates on one hip, his camera on the other. At home in the city he shaved three times a day, but out here among the cedars and piñons he could be himself. Somewhere along the trail his horse had developed a liking for Nusbaum's fifteen-cent straw hat and, in consequence, had eaten two-thirds of the brim. To counterbalance this lack or, more likely, just to annoy his employer, Nusbaum was raising a pair of low-hung sideburns that gave his dark-skinned features, plus the cropped headgear, an elongated appearance precisely matching his horse's face.

Not to be outdone by this engineer-photographer from New Mexico, Kidder began cultivation of a facial covering that soon equaled, or surpassed, every other of its kind known west of the Pecos River. Kidder's beard was light brown in

1 *Bulletin of the University of Utah*, Vol. III, No. 3, Pt. 1 (1910), 2.
2 *American Journal of Archaeology*, Vol. XIV, No. 3 (1910), 337–60.

color, thick and curly, like the mane of a bull bison. That beard, I am sure, would have proven a treasured museum piece on Harvard Square.

There were eleven in the Cummings crew, including two of Kidder's classmates who had stopped off en route to a California vacation to see what archaeology looked like in the raw. The cowboy guide whom they hired at the end of the railroad, knowing only that we were camped somewhere on Alkali Ridge and hoping to find our tracks across the trail, had caused those two young Harvard men to ride thirty-five miles that day, their first on horseback. Both were still alive when they dismounted and, to the surprise of all, were ready for work in a day or two. They stayed on until the end of the season, participating in the daily excavations like men born to the shovel.

The ruin selected for examination, with a conspicuous trash mound at either end, covered approximately three acres. Its rude masonry—roughly fractured stones with mud mortar—had collapsed into a low-lying heap. One trash mound had been searched for burials, with some success to judge from the quantity of scattered bones and broken pottery; the mound at the opposite end awaited exploration. Cedars and piñons crowded in from all sides, but the fallen stonework lay exposed to the hot midday sun. Digging was difficult because of inadequate and insufficient equipment. We were horseback with no space for extras. Nevertheless, seventeen rooms and three kivas were cleared in the course of five weeks. The rest of the ruin was left for future expeditions.

Archaeology as a profession was just feeling its way in 1908, and we were all young and inexperienced. Precision has since replaced the naked eye and a piece of string. New tools and techniques have been put into use—aerial photography, plane tables and alidades, dendrochronology, radiocarbon, pollen and chemical analyses. The students who came afterwards probably described our work as that of "pot-hunters" and "vandals," regardless of the educational institutions we represented. Our errors in observation and recording were honest errors. Our mistakes, like those of our predecessors in field work, served to point the way that eventually led to archaeology as a distinct discipline.

Plodding the sandy mile or more to work every morning was irksome to most of us. So were the long hot hours on pick and shovel. Alkali Ridge in 1908 knew nothing of an eight-hour day, but we were all careful not to work longer than necessary. One fellow, whom we called "Old Mac," did not protest the long days, but he rebelled against carrying a canvas water bag or his share of the lunch. So he always started early and he always got lost, even after blazing the trail with strips from a red bandanna. It was part of my job to go out at daybreak and bring the horses in to water, driving them back again on my way to the ruin. Thus it was that I came to Mac's rescue time and again. It was seemingly impossible for him to follow a trail or to distinguish a human footprint from that of a cow.

Manual labor did not exactly disagree with Old Mac, but it was not his preferred way of life. He had served as United States consul at various posts in Mexico and had made his way north by a succession of stopovers. Having convinced himself that Mother Nature never intended the human body to be incased by air-tight clothing, he fashioned a shirt from a discarded potato sack and went barefoot after losing his carpet slippers. He had joined the Cummings party and accepted temporary work far from town solely to save money. For forty years he had been trying to get back to Chicago to see his old mother, but always there were farewells to

24

exchange with new-found friends. And so it was in 1908: With a ticket in his pocket he lingered for that traditional "one more for the road"—and missed the daily train from Dolores.

Another character on Dean Cummings' crew that year was one whom we knew as "Nick." He talked out of the lower corner of his mouth and smoked endless cigarettes but was always affable and good natured. He was a drifter who required very little in the way of worldly goods and probably signed up for pick-and-shovel work through mis-apprehension. At any rate, from my point of view, Nick was a welcome addition to the company. He took it upon himself to educate Kidder's Harvard friends in the ways of the West. He devised schemes to keep nerves on edge. Old Mac's carpet slippers worn backward left moccasin prints in the trail for all to see next morning. Hoot owls hooting at night were Indians signaling each other; a chance circle, or square, of cedars on the way to work was an undeniable council chamber. Finally, when a Spanish-American trench-ing tool was unsheathed to provide nocturnal protection, Dean Cummings ordered a stop to all monkeyshines. After we parted a few weeks later, Nick practically disappeared. I met him only once more. That was at Farmington, New Mexico, in 1920. He wanted to borrow twenty dollars—"just to tide me over a couple of days."

Upon conclusion of excavations and dispersal of the crew, Kidder and his friends set out for anthropological observa-tions in New Mexico. These were partially realized, so we learned later, when a Mexican at Española stabbed another over a glass of beer. As for Dean Cummings and his two stu-dents, they extended their investigations to the Lower Mon-tezuma and found enough of interest there until it was time to meet John Wetherill in Bluff City.

25

One observation which I thought at the time to be entirely new and unique was the number of prehistoric ruins that included large monolithic stones on end, vaguely reminiscent of the fortified cave dwelling seen in White Canyon the year before. Not until long afterward did I learn that my old friend W. H. Jackson had seen and described these same ruins thirty-three years before.[3]

Aneth, a three-family settlement at the mouth of McElmo Canyon, was the overflow from colonization of Bluff City. As we rode up and dismounted at the low, earth-covered Aneth trading post one day in late July, a man and two women in full Navaho costume arrived with a bundle of sun-dried goat hides. Despite his brown moccasins, his velvet jacket, and his calico pants split to the knee, that man had the features of a Negro and I guessed him to be one.

In answer to my inquiry but perhaps taking advantage of my youthful credulity, the trader said the "black Mexican" was, indeed, a Negro. A onetime hostler attached to a body of passing troops, he had been sold to a local Indian by a pair of waggish soldiers, and now, forty years later, he was the wealthiest Navaho thereabouts—rather an improbable tale, to be sure, but there were the man, his two wives, and the goat hides.

By prearrangement, Professor Cummings met John Wetherill at Bluff City on August 1, 1908, for what was to have been a quick survey of archaeological possibilities in the then little-known northeastern portion of Arizona. Wetherill led the way across the San Juan River at a seldom-used ford about twelve miles downstream and thence through Monument Valley to the comforts of the post-and-mud home he had built for his family two years before.

When Wetherill met Professor Cummings, he was in a

[3] *Tenth Hayden Report* (Washington, 1878), 428.

hurry. His Navaho neighbors were in arms again, this time over orders to send their children to school. Soldiers were coming from Fort Wingate to enforce the order. Women and children had been sent into hiding among the red-walled canyons; men had retrieved their guns from as far away as Cortez and Durango. A fight seemed imminent. Followers of Hoskininni, who had outwitted Kit Carson and his army in 1863, had little fear of Fort Wingate troopers, although the latter had won a brief skirmish near Aneth, Utah, a few weeks before when they arrested By-a-lil-le and nine of his lieutenants. As he had on that occasion, Colonel Hugh L. Scott (later, General; chief of staff under President Wilson), an authority on Indian sign language and army trouble shooter in all Indian disputes, would accompany the soldiers to Oljeto. A conference had been called, and Wetherill wanted to be on hand to defend his Navahos and calm their natural fears in a dispute with soldiers.

We passed the mounted military in Monument Valley just west of Gypsum Creek (whose clear, limpid water was basely deceptive) and learned that they were from various army posts, that they had joined forces at Chinle, at the mouth of Canyon de Chelly, and that they were marching overland to Wetherill's store at Oljeto in Utah, a mile and a half north of the Arizona line. Their numbers were impressive: six troops of cavalry, one machine-gun platoon, fifty pack mules, a wagon train, and all the attendant packers, guides, interpreters, cooks, etc.[4] Lieutenant Colonel George K. Hunter, Fifth Cavalry, Fort Wingate, appeared to be in charge.

The command reached Oljeto on August 4 and deliberately spread its tents broadly across the flat so that the number of men, mules, and equipment could readily be seen. The

4 Report of General Earl D. Thomas, Colorado Headquarters, Denver (September 26, 1908).

conference was to begin three days later. Although Wetherill had been resident among them only two short years, the local Navahos knew and trusted him. They wanted him to talk for them rather than the official interpreters who would be inclined "to talk soldiers' talk."

Washington's orders to send their children to school—and there was no school within two days' horseback ride—did not seem reasonable to the Navahos of Oljeto. They were prepared to question the government order. Nevertheless, the points at issue were readily settled between the leaders even in advance of the meeting, and the threat of hostilities quickly faded. The formal meeting had been set for August 7–9, but two cavalry troops were detached on August 8 to look over the Navaho Mountain region and the Carrizos, while a third, Troop L, scouted the south side of the San Juan as far east as Bluff, returning to Oljeto on August 12. Troop I, sent to the Black Mountain region, got back on August 16.

It was a good conference, successful beyond expectation. Everyone had a chance to orate; arguments on both sides were repeated and repeated again. Finally, after a good meal, partially at Wetherill's expense, all difficulties were resolved and the soldiers went their way. But neither then nor later when I knew him in Washington was I able to understand how Colonel Scott could so quickly win a hostile Indian audience by anecdotes signaled with only three fingers on one hand and perhaps a couple of stubs on the other. Despite this handicap, he was widely known to all Indian peoples, east and west, as "the man who talks with his hands." His unfinished manuscript on the sign language remains at the Smithsonian Institution.

Monument Valley was an incredible, utterly fantastic place when we first saw it on August 2, 1908. A thin Navaho trail

28

crossed through the middle. Sandstone buttes thrust upward one thousand feet, more or less; others, dozens of them, rose hazily in the dim distance. Excepting an occasional, sparrow-like bird startled from its shaded perch beneath a clump of rabbit brush, we saw no living thing, no sign of life. There were no trees on the sandy plain; no shrubs worthy of the name. The valley was empty and silent. Kodachromes add color to current views, but there were no kodachromes in 1908, and our black-and-white snapshots scarcely portray the mystic beauty of the place as we first saw it. Monument Valley was a fairyland then, and it will always remain so despite motels, divided highways, and speeding autos.

When John Wetherill arrived at his new homesite in 1906, a full moon mirrored in a near-by spring gave the location its Navaho name, Oljeto, "Moonlight Water." The country round about was wild and untamed. Local Indians were troublesome and antagonistic. Men wore their hair long and clung to the old ways. Americans were not wanted. Two prospectors had been killed near Navaho Mountain a few years before, and troops were called in. More recently, two other prospectors, Mitchell and Merrick, were killed in Monument Valley, and their killers were still living. Wetherill had been warned not to settle there. Before he could build he had to win permission from Old Hoskininni and his son, Hoskininni-begay, the acknowledged leaders of all who dwelt east of Navaho Mountain.

The home which John Wetherill built in 1906 for his wife and two children was of posts and mud with a dirt roof, curtains at the windows, and Navaho rugs upon the floor. Adjoining the home but separated from it by a stockade fence of cedar posts was a one-room trading post, the first of its kind in far northern Arizona and about 150 roadless miles from wholesale supplies in Gallup, on the Santa Fe Railway.

29

Flagstaff, a later supply point, was an estimated 160 miles distant.

Wetherill's partner, Clyde Colville, was a tall, thin man, whom the Navahos naturally called *Pelicana Naez,* "the tall American." With western adventure in mind he had arrived in Denver from somewhere back east, broke and wearing a derby hat. He was offered a job as clerk in the Hyde Expedition's trading post at Ojo Alamo, a few miles north of Pueblo Bonito. There he became an Indian trader and remained John Wetherill's partner for life. Very little has been written of Clyde Colville. I knew him as quiet, self-effacing, and efficient. He never talked much, but he could do everything else, from plumbing to cooking. He was baby-sitter when the Wetherills were absent; he was guide when need be and guided several parties to Rainbow Bridge after its discovery on August 14, 1909. He was chainman on the William Boone Douglass party surveying Navaho National Monument later that same year.[5]

That show of army strength at the 1908 conference served its purpose but disrupted Dean Cummings' plans for exploration. John Wetherill had been expected to join in search for new ruins, but he had a multiplicity of demands upon his time and was unable to get away. So the Dean and his two students set out by themselves for Segi (Tsegi) Canyon, northwest of Black Mesa, the Segihatsosi, the Adugigei, and other cliff-bordered gorges where unknown caves sheltered Pueblo dwellings and earlier Basket Maker remains. In this canyon country we were quick to learn that centipedes and scorpions took nighttime refuge in shoes and bedding.

One of the first cave ruins we encountered out from Oljeto was appropriately called "The Snake House" for an enormous snake painted across the cave ceiling. Small storerooms clung

[5] G.L.O., Vol. CLXXXII, Utah, 69–70, 138.

like swallow nests to near-by ledges. All had been thoroughly plundered long before; only the ruin remained.

Two caves high on the west side of the Segihatsosi were among those containing evidence of a later prehistoric society superimposed upon that of another. Various pot-shaped holes dug into the compacted-sand floors of such caves may have been designed for food storage, but we found in them only dry bunch grass and shredded bark. One storage bag of cedar bark had closed ends but a lengthwise opening on one side; another bag, knitted of human hair, had been patched with deerskin. There were planting sticks of different shapes and sizes and shovels made of mountain-sheep horn, flattened and tied on the end of a wooden shaft. All these marvelous artifacts, dating back to the beginning of agriculture in the Southwest, were added to the Utah State Museum. It remained for Kidder and Guernsey ten years later to revisit those same caves and provide the data on which current knowledge of the Anasazis and their predecessors is based.

One delightful memory of the Adugigei ("Where She Jumped off the Cliff") is the ten-year-old boy who brought unstrained goats' milk for our breakfast coffee. He would appear on the red rimrock three hundred feet above us just as the morning sun was breaking from cover, pause there a moment on his black pony to bolster courage with a wild trail song, and then make his cautious way down to the uncertainties of our archaeological camp. Like adult Navahos he never walked where he could ride, and he probably never imagined we heard, and thoroughly enjoyed, his morning song from the cliff top. Despite daily visits for a week or more he never trusted us; he was always impatient to get going. We were white men and we were unearthing "the ancient ones."

31

To protect our equipment while explorations were under way, a human skull conspicuously placed upon the pile sufficed for all except Navaho dogs. Edibles, and especially slabs of bacon, had to hang high, out of reach of tree-climbing carnivores. The Segihatsosi was inhabited at that time by scattered family groups of Navahos whose sheep and goats ranged far and wide, but it was the Navahos rather than their flocks that coveted everything in our possession. They would not willingly enter a prehistoric ruin for fear of "the ancient ones," but they had no hesitancy in making off with an unattached knife, a piece of rope, or a scrap of leather from archaeologists. For some reason they were especially partial to anything made of leather.

At the end of his curtailed explorations in the Oljeto area, Professor Cummings returned to the Wetherill home in late August, 1908, and was preparing to leave for Salt Lake City and the university when Mrs. Wetherill related the story of a great stone arch "shaped like a rainbow." She had heard the story earlier in the year from a Navaho acquaintance who was curious to know what Americans were doing in Navaho country.

By way of illustration Mrs. Wetherill had told of the Dean's observations in White Canyon the year before and of the three natural bridges there. It was this recital that had reminded the Indian of a much larger stone bridge in the Navaho Mountain area. He had heard of it but had not seen it. Inquiry was made of every Indian visiting at the trading post. Many had heard of the mysterious stone bridge, but none had actually seen it. Mr. and Mrs. Wetherill had previously planned family visits in southwestern Colorado, and the Utah party decided to accompany them as far as Bluff. However, they promised the Dean to continue their inquiries during the forthcoming winter and to engage as guide

32

anyone who clearly knew the way. Search for the great stone arch "shaped like a rainbow" was definitely on the Cummings program for 1909.

Until that dual trip to Bluff at the end of August, 1908, only John Wetherill and his partner Clyde Colville, Dean Cummings, and half a dozen Navahos whom Mrs. Wetherill had questioned in vain knew of the rumored arch. But, with an overnight stop at Bluff, the story of the new bridge— larger than those which Cummings had surveyed in White Canyon the year before—at once became common knowledge. Residents of Bluff City, with little that was new and novel to talk about, talked about the natural bridge.

III

NINETEEN HUNDRED AND NINE

RETURNING TO OLJETO in the early summer of 1909, Professor Cummings found the Wetherills more intent upon discovering the "rainbow-like" natural bridge over near Navaho Mountain than upon furthering his archaeological explorations. The great stone arch was by this time a reality; it actually existed, and Mrs. Wetherill had talked with one who knew the way.

Following Dean Cummings' request, Mrs. Wetherill had made continuing inquiries, asking her Navaho friends fruitlessly, but finally had learned of two Piutes, father and son, who had seen the arch while hunting strayed horses and could return to it. The son was immediately engaged as guide and a day was fixed when Professor Cummings and John Wetherill would meet him at his hogan in Piute Canyon.

But Dean Cummings, recalling the curtailment of his 1908 plans, was impatient to resume exploration of Segi Canyon, the Segihatsosi, the Adugigei, and other secluded places bordering Skeleton Mesa. So, sometimes under John Wetherill's guidance and sometimes alone, the Dean ventured into almost every rugged corner of the Oljeto country. More than once he encountered opposition from local leaders. Mustachioed Pinietin, who lived over in Neetsin Canyon, was especially pugnacious after an initial friendly meeting. Although white men were not welcome in Navaho territory, the Dean's ever ready smile, his integrity, and his refusal to be pushed around, even by Pinietin, eventually won Navaho

34

recognition and the nickname by which he was thereafter widely known, Natani Yazzie, "Little Captain."

In the middle 1890's, after their collecting successes on the Mesa Verde and in Grand Gulch, Utah, Richard Wetherill and his brother-in-law Charlie Mason had explored the main Segi and partially excavated Keet Seel and lesser cliff dwellings now within Navaho National Monument. Still others, equally noteworthy, remained unknown until Dean Cummings and John Wetherill came upon them. Betatakin, for example, and Inscription House were discovered in early summer, 1909. Wetherill was present as guide and interpreter, but he quite properly recognized Cummings as leader of the party.[1] Wetherill was paid by the day—when he had a day to spare.

KEET SEEL, largest known cliff dwelling in the Southwest, is one I remember for the number of its wattled walls —upright willows bound by horizontal withes, the whole plastered with mud—and especially for the huge spruce log that somehow had been manhandled up the sheer cliff and utilized presumably as support for a front retaining wall. In its prime Keet Seel, filling a cave 350 feet wide, included at least 150 rooms with meandering passageways at the rear. Richard Wetherill and Charlie Mason searched these dark, rear passages for burials. Many individual rooms fronting the alleys were still roofed in 1909 when I scrambled up the sloping cave floor and entered the great ruin. About 1934, so rumor has it, additional excavation and limited stabilization were undertaken with Park Service approval. But, remembering my one and only visit, Keet Seel, "broken pot-

---

1 *The Plateau,* Museum of Northern Arizona, Vol. XXVII, No. 4 (April, 1955), 23–24.

tery" house to the Navahos, remains for me a most remark-able and fascinating cliff dwelling.

INSCRIPTION HOUSE, the one major cave dwelling in Nav-aho National Monument which I never saw, is so named for an inscription carved in the plaster of an interior wall. Chalked-over for photographing, that inscription has been read "1661 Anno Domini" and is supposed to be Spanish, although there are those who question the interpretation. Despite what others have written, that inscription was found by three ten-year-olds, Ben and Ida Wetherill and Malcolm Cummings, accompanying their parents on a first visit to the ruin early in the summer of 1909. William Boone Douglass of the General Land Office later identified himself as the discoverer of both the ruin and its intriguing inscription in his letter of February 2, 1919, to Stephen T. Mather, then director of the National Park Service, and others have made equally unfounded claims. The real discoverers were three children exercising childish curiosity.

LADDER HOUSE, so-called from a ladder of rundles bound to poles with willow withes, was entered by means of a nar-row crack at the right-hand end where upright slabs of sand-stone had settled away from the cliff. Like every other cave ruin we discovered that summer, Ladder House was built on the sloping floor of a cave, and front walls were raised to provide level space in the room next above. Sometimes, but not always, shallow notches had been provided as basal supports for those fronting walls. One of my photographs shows three poles paralleling upper masonry and resting upon protruding beams as though for a balcony, but I am not sure of the identification.

BETATAKIN (Hillside House) is most accessible of the

36

principal ruins comprising Navaho National Monument and is presently Park Service headquarters. It was discovered by Dean Cummings in July, 1909[2] and excavated by him during the following winter.[3] Eight years later, in the spring of 1917, I undertook its partial restoration for the Department of the Interior.

When Professor Cummings first came to northern Arizona in 1908, the main Segi was still known as "Laguna Creek," a name applied back in the 1880's when a succession of fresh-water lakes or ponds marked its course. Ducks and other waterfowl frequented those ponds and the marshes beyond, so the Navahos told us. In the course of time the several pools were joined end to end by a small gully through mid-valley, and as it grew in depth that gully drained the ponds but left their former locations identifiable by intermittent bands of silty humus which showed very plainly in the arroyo banks. Later observers reported fresh-water mollusks in these silt bands, but I saw none.

Below Marsh Pass and its onetime swamps the Segi becomes Tyende Creek and flows northeast to unite with the Chinle and then the Río San Juan. It was here, where Chinle Wash empties into the San Juan, that we forded the river on our way to Oljeto in 1908. The ford provided fairly safe footing for animals when the river was low, but the downstream side broke away sharply and into swimming water. Just beyond, the south bank rose sheer and unscalable. Farther down river, at the upper end of a twisting gorge appropriately called "The Goose Necks," oil possibilities had prompted a north-bank camp named Goodridge. That same campsite was renamed "Mexican Hat," for the dark som-

2 John Wetherill in *ibid.*
3 Byron Cummings, *Indians I Have Known* (Tucson, 1952), 11.

37

brero-shaped caprock on which it stands, when a cable bridge was strung across the river there in the fall of 1909. Fifteen years later we drove our reluctant pack mules across that bridge, swaying like a ribbon in the wind, on our way to the Clay Hills.

Among the Navahos whom we saw repeatedly at Oljeto trading post in 1908 and 1909 were Hoskininni-begay; Sam Chief, a noted medicine man of the period; Huddlechusley, the practical joker; Dogeye-begay; and an old man who stands forth in memory as the one who wore five twenty-dollar gold pieces as buttons for a discarded civilian coat.

Hoskininni-begay was a friend and a frequent guest of the Wetherill family. He was the son and first lieutenant of old Hoskininni, who claimed Mrs. John Wetherill as his grand-daughter. The old man, well on in years when I knew him, was honored and respected by all. His past exploits were widely known and admired. Most notable of these was his escape from Kit Carson and the United States Army in 1863 and 1864.

To put an end to recurrent Navaho raids upon Mexican and Pueblo settlements along the Río Grande and west to the Hopi country, General James H. Carleton in June, 1863, ordered Colonel Carson to capture all Navahos—men, women and children—and destroy their possessions of corn, sheep, and horses. All captives were to be taken to Fort Canby, especially established as a receiving station a few miles north of present-day Ganado, and thence transferred to Bosque Redondo at Fort Sumner on the Pecos River, three hundred miles away in New Mexico. It was a brutal, relentless campaign, but it succeeded. It brought an end to Navaho depredations. Over eight thousand Navahos were taken prisoner and held captive at Bosque Redondo until 1868, when they were released and returned to their home-

"Court House Hotel," in 1907.

Augusta (Sipapu) Natural Bridge, photographed in 1907. Note the lone man on top.

ARCHIVES, OFFICE OF ANTHROPOLOGY, SMITHSONIAN INSTITUTION

Old cable ferry on Grand River near Moab, Utah, in 1907.

The "Old Swing Tree," at Bluff City, Utah, in 1907.

"Aunt Jane" Allen's pioneer home, Bluff City, Utah, in 1907.

Cass Hite, photographed in 1907 by Byron Cummings.

ARCHIVES, OFFICE OF ANTHROPOLOGY, SMITHSONIAN INSTITUTION

Alfred V. Kidder on Alkali Ridge, Utah, in 1908.

Clyde Colville, Mr. and Mrs. John Wetherill and children, and two placer miners from the lower San Juan River, at the Wetherill home, Oljeto, Utah, in 1908.

The soldiers' camp at the Black Mountain Conference, Oljeto,
Utah, in 1908.

"Old Mac" on Alkali Ridge, Utah, 1908.

John Wetherill at Oljeto, Utah, in 1909.

The Keet Seel Ruin, Navaho National Monument, Arizona, in 1909.

The Cummings-Douglass party, searching for a trail across "the slick rocks" on the way to Rainbow Natural Bridge, in 1909.

The first photograph ever taken of Rainbow Natural Bridge,
August 14, 1909.

Byron Cummings, discoverer of Rainbow Bridge, returns to it
in 1935, his seventy-fifth year.

PHOTOGRAPH BY TAD NICHOLS, TUCSON, ARIZONA

Hoskininni, long a leader of the northern Navahos, and wife, at Wetherill's trading post, Oljeto, Utah, in 1909. When Hoskininni died five weeks later, this photograph was blamed for his death.

lands by way of Fort Wingate, the "Bear Springs" of earlier exploring expeditions. Some two thousand escaped capture at the beginning of Carson's roundup, among them Hoskininni and his followers.

As I heard the story at Oljeto, Hoskininni led his family group across the Río San Juan to the security of Grand Gulch and then, still apprehensive, doubled back across the river at the old Piute ford and on to the security of Navaho Mountain. Kit Carson's army, only half-mounted, went wherever Navahos were thought to be but turned back from the flooded San Juan. His Ute scouts, tribal enemies of the Navahos, had a grand time in the campaign stealing horses and women until they got orders to take no more slaves. They lost interest thereafter and gradually drifted back to their sheltered valleys in southwestern Colorado.

The trail that Hoskininni traced around the north and west sides of Navaho Mountain in 1863 is the one which we followed in part to the discovery of Rainbow Bridge in 1909. That trail crept uncertainly over the foothills of the mountain, across cedar-speckled tablelands to a welcome little stream sheltered by pines and aspens, thence over billowing bare sandstone on which unshod horses left no mark, through narrow passes, and down an abrupt sandstone slope where foot-wide steps had been hand-pecked for men and horses. Here, in this empty, unknown region, Hoskininni and his followers escaped Colonel Kit Carson and his soldiers. Here, protected by their sacred mountain and the war god who dwells on its summit, the refugees secluded themselves until all danger of capture had passed. It was a foreign and forbidding land to them; none had been there before.

In 1906, shortly after John Wetherill built his home and trading post at Oljeto, old Hoskininni claimed Mrs. Weth-

39

erill as his long-lost granddaughter, so fluent was her command of his language, and this pseudo-relationship was readily accepted by all in the neighborhood. It was a relationship that reflected advantageously upon Dean Cummings and his party two years later, for all Navahos recognized the Wetherills as their friends and Natani Yazzie was a friend of the Wetherills.

Search for Rainbow Bridge was definitely scheduled for 1909. As agreed, John Wetherill arrived at the Cummings camp in the main Segi in late July, ready and anxious to get started. He also brought the Cummings mail, including word from Kumen Jones in Bluff City that William Boone Douglass of the General Land Office was there en route to Oljeto, with Rainbow Bridge as his objective also.

Although already forty miles out on the trail to Navaho Mountain, Dean Cummings nevertheless insisted upon returning to Oljeto to offer the advantage of his Piute guide, Nasja-begay, whom Mrs. Wetherill had hired in Cummings' name. Turning back from the Segi to wait for the government man annoyed John Wetherill, but he said nothing; after all, he was paid by the day. Together and under Wetherill's guidance, the Cummings and Douglass parties proceeded down Copper Canyon and up the long and dangerous Nokai Mesa trail to Piute Canyon. There, the designated day for Professor Cummings' arrival having passed, Nasja-begay had taken his sheep up the mountain for better grazing. But he was sent for and overtook the dual party two days later in time to lead it through the final labyrinthian miles to Rainbow Bridge, which was reached by the joint expedition about noon on August 14, 1909.

The story of that expedition and the attainment of its goal was first told in *The National Parks Bulletin* (now *The National Parks Magazine*) of November, 1927,[4] and more recently in *Arizona Highways* for August, 1967.[5] Even though white men have usually claimed credit for the discovery and even though Nasja-begay, a Piute Indian who had been there previously, was employed by Professor Cummings as guide, it is still my opinion that success would never have been realized without John Wetherill. With information given by old Nasja in Piute Canyon, John Wetherill found a way through villainous sandstone gorges where there was no trail.

Mr. Douglass, the government surveyor whom Professor Cummings waited for and then credited with joint leadership of the expedition, has persistently claimed that his White Canyon helper, Mike's Boy, was the actual guide to Rainbow Bridge. Circumstantial evidence, however, suggests that Mike's Boy probably got his information in Bluff City some time after the Wetherills and Dean Cummings spent a night there about September 1, 1908. With Mike's Boy in his employ, Mr. Douglass was surveying White Canyon at that time; he first advised the Commissioner of the General Land Office of the reported natural bridge near Navaho Mountain from the new town of Grayson, Utah, on October 7.[6]

After our wearisome, exhausting ride Rainbow Bridge was indeed an inspiring sight. I felt a deep, if momentary, reverence as I stood below that colossal structure, over three hundred feet high and shadowed by cliffs as high again. At the base of the east buttress a small slab-sided altar gave evidence that some unknown Indian in the distant past likewise had offered homage to the Master Builder. Dean Cummings' Navaho wrangler, Dogeye-begay, rode around the arch to our camp on the opposite side because he did not know the prayer to insure his safe return, if he were to pass

4 No. 54.
5 Vol. XLIII, No. 8.
6 File 176521.

beneath. To the Navahos, Rainbow Bridge was a sacred place and, as such, to be respected by all humans.

After we had rested a bit and stretched our legs, I turned to my camera while Don Beauregard and John Wetherill found their way to the summit and there built a monument of sandstone casts from fossil bones of some antediluvian sea monster. Later in the day six of us walked down canyon to the Río Colorado, a raging torrent of muddy water, rather than the silver stream which we expected. Matches lighted our return as long as they lasted, but Rainbow Bridge canyon, only arm's width and incredibly dark in places, is paved throughout with deep pools into which we blindly stumbled. Consequently we were wet, bruised, and cold when we reached camp about midnight, conquerors of the unknown and untried but otherwise satisfied with our adventure.

After the discovery of Rainbow Bridge, Professor Cummings asked me to guide Mr. Douglass and his surveyors to Keet Seel and Betatakin ruins while he and John Wetherill continued their exploration of unnamed canyons south of Navaho Mountain. To carry out this mission, I elected to follow the trail that skirts the east side of the mountain and crosses Piute Canyon well toward its head—the shorter trail which John Wetherill had intended to travel from our Segi Canyon camp a fortnight earlier.

Somewhere along that trail we happened upon a forbidden war ceremony which the Navahos were holding out among the cedars and piñons. Several hundred men were gathered around a huge bonfire singing and dancing backward and forward with short, choppy steps. Such gatherings had been outlawed by the army since Bosque Redondo days, but we did not know this until later. Women were there, too, but in the rear, outside the circle of light. Despite the monotony of it all, the endless repetition of the dancing and singing,

42

we were enjoying the affair as fully as we could until I happened to notice that a couple of dozen young men, all mounted, had quietly drawn a ring around our small group, their horses faced toward us. Perhaps I was unduly nervous, but it seemed a convenient time to make our departure, and I led the way.

Incredible as it may appear to many, we were the first white men ever seen by Navahos in their mid-twenties attending that ceremony—as Hoskininni told Mrs. Wetherill a couple of days later. No other recollection of mine can so accurately measure the isolation of Oljeto in 1909. Subsequently, after reading the army report on the conference held the year before, I learned that Lieutenant Colonel George K. Hunter, of the Fifth Cavalry, Fort Wingate, regarded as "preposterous" a statement that among the two hundred Navahos attending were some who had never before seen a white man. The Colonel was from Fort Wingate, 150 miles distant, but he obviously knew nothing of northern Arizona.

The wife who accompanied Hoskininni to that forbidden ceremony, and later to Oljeto, was blessed with youth and vigor. Three older wives, sisters whom he had previously married, had been left behind with his many slaves. A man of stature in the old days was entitled to service; women and children in addition to less mobile property were frequently captured from Pueblo villages and scattered Mexican settlements. Utes and Navahos were constantly at war with each other, and both took slaves. Hoskininni died five weeks after my picture was taken, and the picture was blamed for his death. Thereafter his family insisted that Mrs. John Wetherill as his principal heir assume responsibility for his thirty-two slaves.

Children and slave women, usually afoot, herded the family sheep and goats. A sheep that could not walk as fast as

43

a horse soon went into the family stew. Thus the first blooded rams introduced by the government were nearly all eaten; improvement of Navaho flocks came later.

As Dean Cummings requested, I guided Mr. Douglass and his party to Keet Seel ruin, left with him a map of the middle Segi showing the location of Betatakin and the Bubbling Spring—two paramount landmarks—and then hurried on to rejoin my companions at Oljeto. Since the Dean, on sabbatical leave from the university, had planned further explorations, our photographer, the artist, and I started home on a short cut through Monument Valley. We were guided by Dogeye-begay, our wrangler on the Rainbow Bridge trip, of whom we were all quite fond. He was a delightful, mild-mannered man with his long, black hair tied in a bun at the back of his neck, his cotton pants split to the knee, his brown velveteen jacket open at the armpits, and silver buttons on his jacket and moccasins. Wetherill had told him to take us to Bluff and left the details to his own ingenuity, even though Dogeye-begay knew no English.

Approaching Bluff City, we found the San Juan in full flood again. Dogeye-begay rose to the occasion and persuaded several Navahos idling near by to carry our cameras, bedrolls, etc. across on their heads; the horses had to swim. While all this was under way, the artist, red haired, tall, and boldly freckled, overcame an inherent modesty by fashioning a personal breechcloth from a red bandanna, much to the amusement of Navaho matrons and daughters gathered upon the bank to witness the crossing.

We three students, non-swimmers all, flung an arm over a cottonwood log which our guide skillfully steered to the opposite shore. Dogeye-begay was a grand fellow and very patient with citified Americans. But he would not permit a picture of himself until I had allowed time for him to put on

44

an old yellow corduroy suit that someone had given him. And next day when I bought food for his return journey, he selected a box of soda crackers and a can of peaches and ate them on the spot, saying, "Easier to carry them that way."

In the fall of 1909, a month or more after our departure, John Wetherill and Clyde Colville moved their trading post from Oljeto to Kayenta, and here Mr. and Mrs. Wetherill built a stone-walled home that became widely famous for its hospitality. Rare bayeta blankets hung from the walls; Navaho rugs carpeted the living-room floor. There were deep, comfortable chairs for all. As the years multiplied, so too did the number of paintings and other treasures, gifts from famous artists and writers. The Wetherill home at Kayenta was far from the railroad, but people somehow heard about it and somehow found the way. Herbert E. Gregory of Yale and the University of Hawaii, A. V. Kidder and S. J. Guernsey of Harvard, T. Mitchell Pruden from New York, and many lesser lights found shelter there. Theodore Roosevelt spent a week at Kayenta in 1913 en route to Rainbow Bridge and back again. He cared nothing about ruins, so he told Wetherill; he "lived for the present and the future." But he would not miss Rainbow Bridge.

After three summers with Professor Cummings in southeastern Utah and northeastern Arizona I continued my apprenticeship under E. L. Hewett, director of the School of American Research at Santa Fe, New Mexico, and then I advanced to the U. S. National Museum, principal unit of the famous Smithsonian Institution. A Civil Service examination opened the door, but it was probably a small skill in freehand sketching rather than my knowledge of anthropological literature that let me in.

IV

AT THE NATIONAL MUSEUM

LOOKING BACKWARD TO MY ARRIVAL in Washington on June 20, 1911, I realize that a more naïve youth probably never came out of the West. There were no desert distances, no cedar trees, no piñons, and no sagebrush. I was listed on the Civil Service records as "Aide, Division of Ethnology" although my museum work then and thereafter was entirely with archaeological material. My initial salary, $75 a month, was the maximum allowed, but this meant less to me then than later. They were doing things at the National Museum!

All about were men of achievement—Charles D. Walcott was secretary of the Smithsonian and a geologist of international renown; W. H. Holmes, my immediate superior, was head curator of anthropology and widely known as artist, geologist, and archaeologist; Walter Hough, curator of ethnology, had but recently succeeded Otis T. Mason, a prolific writer in his field. George P. Merrill was head curator of geology and Leonard Steineger, of biology. W. H. Dall of Alaska fame was daily at the Museum and still studying fossil mollusks after 50 years. Frederick Webb Hodge was at the time ethnologist-in-charge of the Bureau of American Ethnology, and the erudite Marcus Benjamin, editor of National Museum publications. And there were many others, upstairs and down.

As aide in ethnology, my first museum chore—and I remember it well—was unpacking boxes that had been in storage since the Philadelphia Centennial Exposition of 1876.

46

There was box after wooden box, and each disgorged quantities of dusty straw or excelsior packing. Some boxes contained gifts from foreign exhibitors; some contained purchases made with funds briefly available. Stone implements and Mississippi Valley pottery—quantities of both! There were hundreds of stone celts from Puerto Rico—all petaloid celts, one and one-half to eight inches long, pointed- or square-polled—and nothing more precise than "Puerto Rico" for source. I was to classify them.

When the Centennial Exposition had come to its inevitable end, the Exhibits Committee had shipped to Washington every specimen not nailed down and all of the accompanying furniture. These collections—costumes, weapons, and craft products of native peoples the world over; Greek and Roman antiquities; and the cases in which they had been exhibited—were addressed to the Smithsonian Institution. But since the Institution had no space for their display, Congress authorized a special museum (now the Arts and Industries Building), opened to the public in 1881 just in time to be utilized for President Garfield's inaugural ball.

Twenty-five years later much of that 1876 Exposition material was still stored in rented quarters about town, so Congress authorized a second and more up-to-date museum. It was expected that this modern structure would be ready for occupancy by the end of June, 1909, and rental contracts were drawn with that limit in mind. But various building delays intervened, and the occupancy date was advanced and advanced again. Finally, with contracts about to expire, all stored materials were transferred to the new building as fast as floors could be laid in otherwise empty halls.

This "new" National Museum, at the foot of Tenth Street three blocks from Pennsylvania Avenue, faced several squares of wholesale markets. Tenth Street was the natural approach, but crated chickens were piled high on both curbs, calves awaiting slaughter bawled from sidewalk gratings, and a very foul deerhide reeked beneath an east-side awning. Horse-drawn farm wagons with garden produce awaited customers. Wharf pilings of the old Chesapeake-Ohio Canal lay just below the surface.

The new building with over ten acres of floor space had been completed externally in 1910, but the interior plaster was not yet dry when orders came to rush exhibits. It was just at this time that I appeared upon the scene, willing to work but entirely innocent of museum practices.

The "new" National Museum was individualistic, unlike any other. It was entirely up to date. With larger-than-usual exhibition spaces, special furniture had to be designed. In archaeology, for halls with twenty-foot ceilings and windows on both sides, four kinds of cases were provided: those fixed in position against a wall; caster-equipped "floor" cases four feet wide by eight feet long and eight feet high; "double-slope-top" cases with storage drawers beneath; and "narrow flat-top" cases, likewise on rollers and with storage facilities. Each was precisely like every other of its kind, and each was allotted a predetermined space, row upon row. Wall cases and floor cases were equipped with adjustable shelves, but it took two strong men to lift their great, plate-glass fronts. They were all very modern. And every glass-front case was a mirror reflecting every other case and its contents.

Those were parsimonious times at the National Museum. We lacked competent assistants and adequate equipment. But somehow the work was done. Specimens went directly from packing boxes to exhibition shelves, often without dusting. We would await less pressing moments to mark and measure individual objects. As the task progressed, we begged from colleagues in other halls and improvised when other means failed. From sheer necessity we continued to use hand-made pasteboard boxes and trays, salvaged from the "old" museum. Red-stained wooden trays made to fit the old walnut exhibition cases lasted a long, long while. Some are still about. In 1911 the Museum furnished its own heat and its own ice and furnished them at less cost. Billy Knowles and one messenger provided and promptly delivered the office supplies needed from day to day. No other government department presumed to say how Museum activities should be managed.

With ample basement storage space available for the first time in many years, steel racks and drawers were ordered for the heavier stone specimens in geology and anthropology. But the contractor who submitted a low bid on the steel racks was too high in his bid for the accompanying drawers. Consequently, two bids were let, one for racks and one for drawers. And the low-bid storage drawers, too narrow and too light in weight for their intended purpose, buckled and dropped off runners in the low-bid racks. I do not know how much our administrators saved on that transaction, but forty years passed before the last of that ill-advised purchase was surreptitiously replaced.

Commiserating with me over our joint storage problems, and for years thereafter, old "Ike" Millner, an aide in the department of geology, was an always welcome visitor to my crowded laboratory. His interest in archaeology was limited to those small discards that would serve to illustrate his impromptu talks to Boy Scouts and similar groups. He had an uncommonly easy way with children and an endless variety of stories to tell. A Union seaman during the Civil War and a lookout on Farragut's flagship at the battle of New Orleans, his tales of wartime adventures and his escapades while foraging Confederate farms for food fascinated

49

adults, myself included, no less than children. As a prisoner at Andersonville, he had traded jacket buttons to Confederate lieutenants for peanuts to supplement a sparse menu—Union buttons were especially prized by Southern belles of the period—and his Yankee ingenuity had fashioned into spoons for generous dipping occasional beef horns salvaged from the camp stewpot. In prewar days "Ike" was a helper at his father's shipyard on the Hudson below Albany, and there had become acquainted with Brigham Young, then a stevedore about the docks but afterward the great Mormon leader.

Eventually Millner retired from daily work and moved to South Carolina to live with a son. A few years later when I called there to see him, he was crowding each day with what he enjoyed best, teaching children—this time teaching blind children from a near-by school the differences between varieties of local flowers.

Gentle I. M. Casanowicz, an authority on the Bible and formerly in charge of the section on religions, was made responsible for our Old World collections—paleolithic stonework from Scandinavian countries, Greek and Roman antiquities, scarabs and mummy cases from Egypt—when these were moved to the new building. His diverse exhibits crowded a huge, second-floor hall and an alcove overlooking the north entrance. Two items from the former section on religions, models of the Mormon Temple and Tabernacle in Salt Lake City, gifts from the Church of Latter-day Saints following the Seattle exposition, were charged to my division of archaeology because, I can only surmise, I was a graduate of Utah University. The division was a receptacle for discards—anything not wanted elsewhere was sent unquestioned to archaeology.

Three halls with 216 exhibition cases on nearly 35,000

square feet of floor space were reserved for Western Hemisphere archaeology—from the Arctic to the Antarctic. Under Professor Holmes's supervision, those 216 cases were my responsibility; filling them in a hurry, my job. Stone implements and pottery from Mississippi Valley mounds—the harvest of field work in the 1880's—predominated among the collections which we unpacked on the cement floor of the new museum building. There was no time to mark and describe individual specimens. They were unpacked and immediately put in exhibition cases, and the contents of those cases became visible storage not to be changed appreciably for forty years.

My only assistant for this 1911 undertaking and for the accompanying laboratory work (or as much of it as we could manage at the time) was a Civil War veteran who had joined the staff in 1878 as aide to the late Charles Rau, then curator of archaeology, and had remained in the division thereafter. He was a delightful companion, calm and unhurried, and a musician of considerable ability. He played a violin in the old Georgetown orchestra; at the Museum he was frequently called upon to solve problems relating to musical instruments. And every month, two days after payday, he borrowed fifty cents for carfare.

Although employed as an aide in archaeology, my assistant was not particularly interested in the subject. But he was a very agreeable colleague and blessed with a remarkable memory. Trained in the cramped quarters of the 1881 museum where space was always at a premium, he had the fortunate faculty of being able to remember exactly where he put things, even parts of a single accession. With no time to mark and describe individual specimens, the requisite catalog number was commonly penciled on a scrap of paper and placed

51

with the material to await a more favorable opportunity—an opportunity that never came. He kept no storage record, but he accounted for every moment of the working day.

At some unknown time in the past some forgotten administrator had issued an edict requiring every member of the staff to note his every daily activity. Fulfillment of this chore had become an obsession with my elderly assistant: three minutes for a drink of water at the cooler down the hall; thirty-two for lunch; seven for a trip to the toilet. Death finally brought an end to this meticulous listing of moments, and thereafter I quietly discarded his reams of yellow-leaf tabulations. No one, to my knowledge, had ever bothered to consult them.

In his later years failing health reduced the old gentleman's activities, and a Negro, Charles T. Terry, Jr., was employed as probational aide to mark specimens—the first to break the segregation barrier in our division of archaeology. From this beginning my nonwhite assistant gradually advanced to become an indispensable member of the organization. He not only numbered specimens but kept our records of the study collections so that any given object, if called for by a visiting scientist, could be brought to the laboratory with minimum delay. But he was of no help in the description and classification of materials; he just did not know archaeological materials. This never ending task of classification and description was supposed to take precedence, but it had been neglected throughout the years and inadequately accessioned collections allowed to accumulate. The advice which I received repeatedly was to follow the established practice: relegate incoming material to the background, and concentrate on research and publications. It just happened I was not built that way: Work to be done was there to do.

The present generation of federal employees has forgotten,

if it ever knew, that working days were once longer. In 1911, for instance, there were eight full hours in a day and six days in a week, except during July, August, and September when Saturdays were reduced to four hours. Not until 1932 was there talk of a five-day, forty-hour week. Administrators simply worked a man until he could work no longer.

"Old Man" Murphy, for example, had been handed down from the past. I never did learn his history, but he had been around a long while and his clay pipe had caused a dark lower-lip tumor. Time had laid such a heavy hand upon Murphy that he had been detailed to dusting exhibition cases whether they were in need of dusting or not. And here he spent his hours, polishing slowly down the length of the hall and back again. Each year on St. Patrick's Day our Murphy would bedeck himself with an orange-colored necktie or boutonniere and belligerently watch for the green ribbon his old eyes could not see.

There was a time when the National Museum prided itself upon spotless exhibition cases, free from the imprints of sticky little hands and adult noses. In the archaeological halls, at least, this cleaning job was one for "the bull gang," five husky Negroes who worked as a unit and found justifiable self-satisfaction in their results. Our big floor cases, each with its three-hundred-pound plate-glass side panels, offered individual challenges despite their similarity. Two men would lift out the heavy glass and support it while the others cleaned. As they went about their daylong task these men frequently broke into song, country hymns sung with all the rich resonance and harmony of a church organ. Museum visitors stopped at a distance to listen, and I shall always believe we lost something unique and distinctive when "the bull gang" was discontinued.

A couple of years after coming to Washington, I concluded that further schooling was desirable and enrolled at the local university for a course in Greek archaeology under Professor Mitchell Carroll. When the latter triumphantly told Professor Holmes of my enrollment, Holmes remarked, with a knowing twinkle in his eye, "It will probably do him no harm." Not until several months later did I realize the full significance of that remark.

W. H. Holmes habitually wore a sharp Vandyke beard. That graying beard, his keen brown eyes, and a natural aloofness made him seem taciturn and brusque to many. On the contrary, he was warmhearted and friendly, even jovial in a quiet sort of way. Schooled as a teacher, he became a self-made master of the English language. Everything he wrote was clear, precise, and to the point; his monographs on archaeology have never been surpassed. Artist, geologist, and archaeologist all in one, Holmes served with the Hayden Surveys in the middle 1870's, thereafter with the U.S. Geological Survey and the Field Columbian Museum, Chicago. About 1896 he was persuaded to return to Washington as head curator of anthropology at the U.S. National Museum, and from this office he was appointed in 1902 to succeed Major John Wesley Powell as director of the Bureau of American Ethnology. Administering the Bureau, however, was not to his liking, and he was doubtless glad to return to the Museum seven years later, first in his former position as head curator, Department of Anthropology, and then as the first director of the newly established National Gallery of Art (now the National Collection of Fine Arts).

By 1914 it seemed essential that I obtain specialized training in the American field, so I went prospecting for Ph.D. possibilities. California, standing high in anthropological instruction, was out of the question for I had just crossed the continent; at the University of Chicago, Prof. Frederick Starr

54

offered a course in Mexican archaeology during alternate semesters and that was all. Professor Franz Boas at Columbia was teaching linguistics only, and I was not interested in Indian languages. Harvard, most promising of all, appeared too expensive for my purse, and I lacked the wisdom to borrow.

By this recital I desire merely to direct attention to the fact that, of the universities investigated in 1914, only four were offering courses in American anthropology leading to the doctorate, while today there are fifty-five, plus four more in Canada. During 1964–65, these universities awarded 161 doctorates in anthropology alone.

One day I was called into the head office and introduced to a Dr. Frederick Wilhelm von Alpenstock, or something of the sort, professor of archaeology at the University of Leipzig. On this, his first visit to Washington, would I kindly show him our Museum collections and some of the more important federal buildings? With his broken English and my four years of college German we got on very well together. The Museum tour did not take long since he was not interested in American antiquities and we had absolutely nothing from the Fino-Ugrian area on the Russian border.

In late morning our guest remarked that it was nearly lunch time and invited me to join him. At his hotel, on Fifteenth Street overlooking the U. S. Treasury, he ordered, not the sandwich that would have sufficed, but a whole roast chicken for each, golden brown and fresh from the oven, and a pitcher of beer. Luncheon lasted a good two hours with much talk of Germany, its unique geographical features, and its universities. I admitted a desire to take my doctorate abroad, preferably under his tutelage. Then without warning, he announced that he was accustomed to midafternoon rest and relaxation. Could I suggest a quiet beer garden?

Geyer's place out on Fourteenth Street seemed to meet the requirement. Its tables were screened by a high board fence and sheltered by spreading elms; music played softly in the background. Only the best people went there, including the Swiss editor of a German bi-weekly. Two pints of beer filled the afternoon, and I confess that my mental image of Germany was by then a patchwork of divers colors, blurred at the edges. I had no strength to resist when Dr. von Alpenstock remembered the desirability of a brief rest before dinner. Would I suggest a first-class restaurant and join him?

We went to Gerstenberg's, on the north side of the Avenue and just around the corner. Here two huge *Wiener Schnitzels* were called for *mit Kartoffeln, und Kraut und zwei seideln Bier.* The Herr Professor and I parted with expressions of mutual admiration, and I vowed to join him at his university just as soon as I could save passage.

But then came World War I and transatlantic transportation was free. I enlisted in the Air Corps but never saw Leipzig. And I never saw my German professor again.

During Air Corps training I was quartered for a time in one of the ivy-covered quadrangles at Princeton University —a circumstance that enabled me later to identify myself as a "Princeton man." Various incidents shine out from those weeks in training, including the night I stood guard duty. It was a Saturday night and everyone had to check in before eleven. But along toward midnight half a dozen roisterers came noisily down the boardwalk from town. Hearing the racket, I reversed my lonely beat and reached the front corner of the building just as the guard at the entrance called out: "Halt! Who goes there?" Silence prevailed for a few seconds and then a single response: "Jesus Christ and the twelve apostles." "Advance and be recognized." At that challenge

56

the O.D. descended the stairway in a flurry, and duty abruptly called me to the far rear end of my accustomed path.

While I was absent in 1918, my old Civil War assistant died and was replaced by an aide from the department of zoology whose position there had been abolished because he appeared to be less interested in zoology than in erecting sailing ships inside small-necked bottles. Once in archaeology his major interest reverted to zoology, or at least to herpetology, for he began raising constrictors as a hobby and often kept one or more five-footers, safely boxed, in the division laboratory, to the apprehensive terror of the cleaning women. Despite his fluctuating enthusiasms my new aide had more than average skill as a draftsman and was helpful as such. But his transfer provided further evidence that, administrators to the contrary, not every individual could adjust himself to the routine of an archaeological laboratory.

This conclusion was shared, I have reason to know, by my superior, Walter Hough, who had succeeded W. H. Holmes as head curator of anthropology. Like Holmes, however, Hough was too easily persuaded by others; he lacked courage to protest unwise and ill-conceived orders. He was a student primarily, possessed of an encyclopedic mind and interested in all things anthropological. When he retired in 1935 after fifty years at the National Museum, there were still numerous facets of human culture awaiting his attention, and he expected to undertake each in its proper turn.

Office procedure for a long time required that replies to official letters be initiated with a curator's penciled memo, then sent to the head curator for approval, and thereafter to the chief clerk for literary composition and typing. However, Smithsonian personnel in charge of the National Museum seemed unable to realize that those initial memoranda often called for more than the mere ability to write. Some entailed considerable searching not only in our records but in the libraries. At least twice during summer-long absences my curatorial salary was paid in full to an arrowhead collector called in as a replacement. What he could not readily manage each day was set aside to await my return in the fall. Those who had made the appointment never considered the night work necessary to bridge the omissions, and night work was often necessary and Sunday work too.

Again, in 1924 while I was in the field, a "War Portrait Gallery"—oil paintings of "Veterans Fifty Years after the Civil War"—was intruded into my North American archaeological hall, occupying 1,225 square feet of floor space and compelling retirement of fifteen exhibition cases. The person who ordered that substitution did not trouble, so far as I know, to return to pass judgment upon the change, but the portraits eventually were replaced by something else and, finally, by an assorted Chinese collection. A museum, apparently, was only a place to hang things.

It was this decision-making by those who had little knowledge of, and little interest in, our archaeological problems that proved so annoying and discouraging. "You had a thousand trays last year. Why do you need more now?"

The analysis and cataloguing of collections are museum chores which most people, myself included, dislike. They are time-consuming chores and they deny one more rewarding activities. It is research that sharpens the intellect. I was all for field work and so were my superiors, but someone had to do the drudgery.

At the National Museum cataloguing of anthropological materials began on March 9, 1859, upon transfer from the National Institute of the vast collections made in the Far East by Commodore Matthew C. Perry, U.S.N., and the U.S.

Exploring Expedition under Lieutenant Charles Wilkes. The original catalog books were nine- by fourteen-inch ledgers with items listed one after the other, irrespective of size and origin. On November 30, 1876, some nameless recorder with sketching ability began the practice of inserting individual drawings beside the book entry. That practice waxed and waned over the years, but those hurried sketches have been the means of identifying many invaluable specimens that might otherwise have been lost to history.

Back in 1906 orders had come to substitute individual catalog cards for the ledger entries and to make the record full. But, no provision was made for additional help to do the additional labor. In consequence and because there was no alternative, I spent many a night hour at the Museum and many a Sunday typing out the essential data with two forefingers. It was 1918 or 1919 before even a part-time typist was allowed; temporaries had to suffice for several years following. Three temporaries were employed during fiscal 1923, and then the division got its first permanent typist on June 7. It was a long wait.

Meanwhile, to help balance the lack of personnel we adopted the custom of encouraging high-school students to study archaeology with us on Saturdays and during summer vacations—a custom that has its reward today in the number of those former students now occupying positions of high responsibility in museums and universities.

In 1934 the Works Progress Administration sent us a number of unemployed who, largely owing to my own insufficiency, proved less helpful than was expected. A former minister in the group, a onetime tourist guide in Greece, felt equal to the occasion and daily countered my instructions—for a time. After this W.P.A. crew left—and they were withdrawn without warning—months passed before order was

59

restored and misplaced study collections were returned to their assigned places. It was this W.P.A. period, perhaps, that introduced into government service and elsewhere the necessity of hiring three people to do the work of one.

In the foregoing, with thoughts going back to the days when I worked almost alone, I have perhaps complained unduly—of inadequate equipment, of administrators who lacked appreciation of the specialized activities they administered, of miserly appropriations, and of a too-limited personnel in office and laboratory. There were scant funds for original research, none at all for attendance at scientific meetings. More recently conditions have changed for the better, not in consequence of my complaints, I am sure, but as a result of wiser men at the top and in recognition of the fact that out-of-the-ordinary tasks are best performed by one who knows what to do.

Beginning about 1930 college-trained men were added to the staff one by one, and competent laboratory aides were found to help process incoming collections. Then, after thirty-nine years at the same desk and on the same museum chores, the urge to complete long-neglected reports on past field work became overwhelming, and I left the curatorship to younger and more capable hands.

As indicated above, my first four years at the National Museum had been devoted largely to salvaging archaeological collections previously received. After this four-year apprenticeship or, more likely, because $500 then available would revert to the Treasury at the end of June, I was invited by the Bureau of American Ethnology in the early spring of 1915 to investigate the so-called "Spanish diggings," reported along the Niobrara in eastern Wyoming. It did not take long to discover that the "diggings" had nothing to do with Spanish explorations but were merely outcroppings of fine-grained quartzite where Indian craftsmen had quarried material for arrowheads and knives. Getting to and from the site was what made my first Smithsonian field trip a memorable experience.

From Cheyenne a string of ore cars made the night run to Ironton, a small hillside mining town where I was to engage a team and driver. One passenger car at the rear was partially heated by a large, pot-bellied stove; the forward two-thirds was cold. At Ironton a foot of frozen snow covered the ground; streets were empty and the "hotel" dark. Sympathetic to my inexperience, the train brakeman showed me how the town operated. At the untended hotel I took a kerosene lamp from the desk and a key from the rack and found my way to a numbered room. There was ice in the water pitcher next morning.

From "the Spanish diggings," instructions took me to northern Utah where "Indian remains" had been reported near Willard, on the northeastern shore of Great Salt Lake. With expenses limited to $500 from Washington out and back again, excavations necessarily were little more than test pits. But the floor of a circular structure was exposed, a rimmed fireplace in the middle and four roof-supporting posts at the quarters. Burned adobe bearing imprints of reeds and willows identified the over-all covering. Discarded stone implements and potsherds spotted the surface.

If I gave less than expected attention to my work, it was because local strawberries were ripe—the most luscious strawberries in the whole world, especially when floated in rich Jersey cream.

However meager my findings at Willard, they led to more illuminating discoveries later. Mr. Don Maguire, a mining engineer then living in Ogden, had traveled the length of Utah between 1880 and 1900 gathering antiquities for his

61

own amusement and for the Chicago World's Fair of 1893. Following his trail from north to south, I revisited some of the prehistoric village sites he had partially excavated and came upon many others.

The prehistory of western Utah is virtually unknown. It was unknown in 1915 when I began my studies there and it remains unknown today, or nearly so. One may comb the reports of early explorers and learn what they saw; one may interrogate present-day farmers; and one may dig for first-hand information. But the whole story has not yet been disclosed. Down the length of western Utah between the mountains and the deserts, suitable building stone is generally lacking, and here the ancients built with mud. Most of their homes were one-room rectangular structures; a few were round or almost round. They were grouped several dozen or more, to form haphazard settlements usually on the crest of a low elevation but not too far from fresh water.

Salt Lake City overlays the remains of such a settlement. That famous explorer of the early West, Ferdinand V. Hayden of the U. S. Geological Survey, found fragments of pottery "4 feet below the surface," and I saw equally convincing evidence fifty years later. Edward Palmer, collecting for the Smithsonian Institution between 1868 and 1875, once turned from his intended path to examine adobe dwellings near Payson at the south end of Utah Lake. In one of those dwellings "prehistoric" wheat capable of a ten-fold yield had allegedly been found "sealed in a stone box," but the sharp-eyed Palmer, examining the evidence at first hand, concluded the wheat was no more than gleanings of a busy, present-day field mouse and the "stone box," its storage place under an adobe wall. Palmer's observations were published at the time by that worthy institution, the Davenport Academy of Sciences.

Don Maguire and Professor Henry Montgomery, the latter from the University of Utah, had both excavated at Paragonah in 1893. Montgomery's modest collection, when I saw it, was housed on the west side of Salt Lake City, in a three-story building then part of the state university but years later converted into the city's West Side High School. From all I could gather, western Utah was an unknown and virtually unreported archaeological field. I decided to have a look at it, and the looking continued for five years.

My extended observations were begun at Beaver, a charming tree-shaded village in a lower west-side county of the same name, and one of those which Maguire and Montgomery had missed. My introduction was through a Beaver resident, a university student whose verbal description placed a once considerable settlement near by—"hundreds" of earth mounds, most of which had long since given way to the plow and modern agriculture. Each mound consisted of wind-blown accumulations about the adobe walls of a prehistoric dwelling.

Of the dozen or so mounds that remained in 1915 I cleared about half, inside and out, and learned that each covered the remains of a residence whose walls were entirely of adobe mud. The mud had been laid in layers ten to twelve inches thick and of wall width, the mud in each layer just firm enough to support its own weight. So constructed, the walls dried out as they rose to ceiling height. Wind-deposited earth had settled against the exterior, and as it accumulated a fine fabric of rootlets from surface vegetation formed between the made walls and the aeolian deposits. Struck upward from below, as we soon learned, these aeolian deposits separated readily along the rootlets and left house walls standing free.

Of all the rooms we cleared, not one was provided with a lateral doorway, thus it was obvious that entrance had been

63

through the roof. Windows and other small wall openings likewise were lacking. All light entering the room came through the ceiling doorway. There was no means of ascertaining the hatchway position, but sandstone disks approximately thirty inches in diameter by two inches thick, found on the floor of several houses, identified the probable hatchway covering. And only one to the house!

My host during this examination, Ambrose McGarry, was a student with whom I had previously planned a vacation-time reconnaissance of the eastern margin of Escalante Desert. From Beaver we were to proceed southward to Paragonah, in Iron County, where Don Maguire and Professor Montgomery had excavated in January, 1893, thence to St. George—Utah's "Dixieland"—in the extreme southwestern corner of the state, then east to Kanab and back to Beaver. But, unknown to me, McGarry had invited a favorite professor to join him on the trip. To this I could not seriously object since "Brose" was furnishing a team and doing the driving without charge; his guest, a small man, fitted snugly into our one-seat buggy.

Paragonah and its nearest neighbor, Parowan, are two small towns that loom large in the history of west-central Utah. They stand beside the old California trail and were settled shortly after Brigham Young and his pioneer followers reached Salt Lake City in 1847. Both are believed to have participated in the Mountain Meadows massacre ten years later; both furnished colonists in 1876 for Arizona settlements along the little Colorado River and, three years later, for the founding of Bluff City, our haven on the Río San Juan in 1907, 1908, and 1909.

The old California trail, still a dirt road in 1915, has since been replaced by U.S. 91, a high-speed thoroughfare that leads from Salt Lake City south through Beaver and Cedar

64

City to provide access to those scenic wonderlands, Zion and Bryce National Parks and Cedar Breaks National Monument. We had scant thought of speeding autos as we trotted south along that dusty road in 1915, but they are there now.

From Parowan my companions and I turned off course for examination of aboriginal inscriptions at "Hieroglyphic Gap" and an expected night camp at Rush Lake. However, as we approached the lake just at dusk, we were met by such hordes of undernourished mosquitoes that the horses refused to drink; therefore we continued and made an after-dark camp in a barnyard at the little town of Enoch. An irrigation ditch flowed along the barnyard fence. A small fire furnished light and a can of beans, our supper. Seeing the fire, the owner came out to investigate and sat there on his heels, a smallish man with gray beard and no teeth poking at the barnyard accumulation with a stick while supper was in preparation. We talked of this and that: local schools and the university, the price of beef and the mosquitoes at Rush Lake. Suddenly and without warning, the professor asked: "Mr. Jones, what do you know about the Mountain Meadows massacre?" Mr. Jones dropped forward onto his knees, reached out to rap his questioner sharply with the stick, and said: "Not a god-damned thing." This was strong language for a Mormon, but it abruptly ended an unwelcome interrogation.

At St. George, known affectionately throughout Utah as "Dixie, the land of milk and honey and good red wine," I really came into my own. We registered at the local hotel, operated by a family of Judds, and because of this circumstance the three of us had the best the hotel offered. The town was full of Judds, including several very substantial citizens. Our proprietor introduced a Mr. R. A. Morris, sole survivor of the three-man crew that assisted Edward Palmer in 1875 when he turned an irrigation ditch into an Indian burial

65

mound in near-by Santa Clara Canyon and thus, without physical work, exhumed a collection of prehistoric pottery. I was especially interested in this chance meeting, for part of Palmer's pottery had gone to the National Museum and I had placed it on exhibit and sought in vain for related notes. Palmer was one of those busy individuals who trusted his memory. Such notes as he kept were scrawled on scraps of paper—any handy scrap—and were absolutely illegible. When he and his memory passed on, such notes as were made of the Santa Clara excavations, if any, passed on also, and only the pottery now remains.

After breakfast next morning the three of us set out for Kanab, following a saddle-horse trail. At that time there was no road worthy of the name between St. George and Kanab; we followed the trail when possible, but new fences restricted travel. It was a rough ride, and the little professor may have regretted his position between two larger men. At upper Short Creek, an area later newsworthy for its hidden polygamists, we stopped to inquire about ruins from a man whose only home for a wife and eight-year-old daughter was a one-room dugout in the bank of an arroyo. Their drinking water came from a vile-smelling seep below the roots of a cottonwood. Wife and daughter watched dubiously from the darkness of their home as we queried the man of the house.

Farther down valley we camped for the night at Galligher's ranch where a windmill advertised water. Young Galligher and his mother, from Missouri as I recall, had been tricked into buying worthless land "because there were no trees to cut down." They had enough money left to string a one-wire fence around an acre of corn, but range cattle had crawled under and eaten the green crop. One of his two horses had died a few days before, thus limiting his plans for the season. Antelope Valley, their new homesite, was rimmed on the

66

north by sandstone cliffs; on the south, it drained into the Grand Canyon. Barren and treeless, the valley was hot in summer and probably cold in winter. With no neighbors nearer than the man in the dugout and his family—at least we saw no other—Galligher's place seemed very remote.

As we sat in the light of a small brush fire chatting with our host and his mother, both lonely for conversation, Andy Siler and his wife rode up and dismounted. A onetime cowboy from House Rock Valley, Siler was returning his wife from vacation. He had ridden out to the railroad a couple of days earlier and had "cut every goddamned fence on the trail." He had been riding that trail for thirty years; "wasn't going to let any goddamned farmer shut him out." Andy had strong feelings and did not hesitate to express them. Like ourselves, he and his wife had stopped there because the Galligher windmill gave promise of water, and water was always hard to come by in Antelope Valley. Together, we shared a supper of baking-powder biscuits, bacon gravy, and coffee and eventually spread our individual bedrolls on the bare ground and went to sleep.

Early next morning as we were preparing to leave, his wife on one horse and her bags on a third, Andy was still cursing the treeless country, the new settlers, and cattlemen who didn't keep track of their cattle. But he turned to our overnight host and I heard him say: "Here, boy, you can't plow with one horse. Go over to my pasture and pick out a good horse; use it as long as you want to and then put it back."

Pipe Spring, between Short Creek and Kanab, is now a National Monument, but its restoration postdates our noontime stop in 1915 when its spring water and the shade of its sheltering trees were both welcome. Its two sandstone buildings, once joined by heavy doors to form an open court and with portholes at the second-story level, were built about

67

1870 as protection against raiding Navahos. At that time, according to "Old Brig" Riggs, one of the early settlers, Indians knew the place as "Yellow Rock Spring." Young Navahos used to ford the Colorado either at the mouth of the Paria or at "the Crossing of the Fathers," farther up river, and run off Mormon horses and cattle. While younger men braved a tribal taboo against crossing the great river, their elders would not. Nevertheless, young or old, Navahos had been fording the river on those old Ute trails ever since Mormons settled the Kanab district, and they made a particularly costly attack in 1864. Ute Indians on hunting or trading expeditions to the west had mapped the trails; Navahos came later, using the same paths.

In and about Kanab we learned of various prehistoric ruins, but time and money were running out and we hurried along. A year or two before our visit, flood waters roaring down Kanab Creek had undermined one such ruin in the yard of a west-side residence. Another, two miles to the north, was razed in 1911 when the town reservoir was built. Rumors of many other ruins, large and small, and of caves in the lower reaches of Kanab Canyon sharpened my curiosity and left me with a resolve to see that little-known region thoroughly at first opportunity. Local residents were a friendly, hospitable people, and their offers to aid in my researches seemed genuine enough. However, one could not expect them to work for nothing, and my available funds were in short supply.

The following year, 1916, I returned to learn more of the prehistoric settlers of Paragonah, a community reported by Maguire and Montgomery and still earlier government explorers to have included "several hundred" mounds. In the course of a few weeks we razed more than twenty of these mounds—almost the last of their kind—and found each concealing a house quite like those uncovered at Beaver, despite individual differences in size and construction. Also, there were roundish rooms that might, conceivably, have been protokivas or prestandardized ceremonial chambers. Further, there were open courts between the rooms and open hearths in the courts. Apparently the prehistoric builders of these primitive structures lived a considerable portion of their daily lives in these open courts, presumably with shelters above the hearths.

Several of the mounds which we opened were located on property of a newcomer, possibly a recent convert to Mormonism. He and his wife and a grown son lived in a two-room house with a huge open fireplace at one end and a loft overhead where the son slept. I judged that they were recent arrivals, perhaps from Tennessee or Kentucky, because both parents used tobacco, frowned upon by orthodox Mormons. Repeatedly at the end of the day's work, I stopped in to chat and smoke a pipe with them—both smoked corncob pipes and simultaneously chewed longleaf—while supper was cooking in an iron kettle hung from a fireplace bracket.

This 1916 season at Paragonah was the longest and most informative of all those spent in western Utah, and, toward the end of it, I received a gratuitous lesson I shall never forget. While work was in progress one day, freeing house walls and floors and dragging away the residue with horse-drawn scrapers, I was hailed by one of our frequent visitors, an elderly gentleman who always occupied the same place over next the fence and sat there on his heels hour after hour without a word. When he finally spoke, it was to the point. "Young feller," he said, "what do you expect to find here?" I explained our purpose as best I could. "How much is it costing?" I made a rapid calculation: three teams at five dollars each; ten men at two dollars—"about thirty-five dollars a day."

69

"It's a waste of money," the visitor said. "Go down to the Co-op store and buy the Book of Mormon. It will cost about four bits and it will tell all you need to know."

Following Paragonah, I turned inland across the Escalante Desert and north over what was known locally as "Black Rock Desert" toward a vast area of brushless land then being developed for agriculture. From past experience I expected to find the adobe houses of prehistoric farmers in this vicinity, and I was not disappointed. A single day's horse-and-buggy survey of the new farming communities surrounding Abraham, Hinkley, Deseret, and Oasis showed that these flat acres had been at least partially cultivated. Low mounds marked the crumpled remains of earth-walled dwellings.

My day ended at Oasis on an unhappy note. A young couple had rushed in from the country with a two-year-old boy choking with whooping cough and had hurriedly occupied a corner of the second-floor lounge at the local hotel. Their preferred physician being out on another case, a substitute was called in the emergency. With other helpless transients I heard the preferred physician arrive tardily, only to turn and leave with an exclamation at sight of the substitute. The Hippocratic oath and medical ethics were upheld that afternoon, but we lost the boy.

Next I caught the mail stage for Fillmore to look at some newly reported ruins a few miles to the south. The ruins were there all right—another remnant of a once extensive settlement of ancient earth-walled dwellings. But of equal interest was the fact that here I unexpectedly crossed the trail of an old-timer whom I knew only by hearsay, Dr. Edward Palmer. A Civil War physician or surgeon, Palmer later abandoned medicine in favor of biology and botany, collecting principally for the Smithsonian Institution and the Peabody Museum of Harvard. He collected everywhere, all over the

70

United States and all over Mexico. I had cared for some of the pottery which he had washed out of a burial mound near St. George in 1875; I had also tried, unsuccessfully, as I have related, to assemble his scattered field notes regarding that and other collections. During my reconnaissance of southwestern Utah in 1915 I met R. A. Morris, one of the three men who had assisted Dr. Palmer forty years before, and the meeting brought the Civil War physician within the field of my acquaintance.

It is reported that on one of his southern campaigns Palmer's tent was appropriated by a cat with a family of kittens; that he seized each rodent the cat brought in, added its skin to his collection, and returned the naked carcass for the kittens. Like the cat, he was a tireless collector and let nothing escape.

At the time of my visit to Fillmore, Dr. Palmer was still remembered by at least one citizen as "the bug man." "He nailed every lizard he saw and grabbed every insect and usually had his pockets bulging with such stuff." My informant said that Dr. Palmer traveled in an army ambulance with a squad of soldiers from Fort Douglas, situated at the foot of the mountains east of Salt Lake City. As a matter of fact, there was no need for the military escort since Utah Indians of that period, however troublesome to settlers, always made way for the man who seemed a little queer.

Relics from the ancient Indian farming community on the south edge of the village were displayed, along with utensils and costumes from pioneer days, in the old capitol building, erected in 1851 to house the territorial legislature. The history of Fillmore begins with the very beginning of Utah history.

Six or eight miles farther south is a basalt-walled cove that had served as a picnic ground in early days. Pavant

71

Indians, it was said, had quarried obsidian here for arrowheads and knives; meaningless inscriptions resembling those at Hieroglyph Gap west of Parowan had been pecked upon the basalt outcroppings. Indian burials, it was also said, had occasionally been found among the rocks by the picnickers.

A year or two after my Fillmore sojourn I was back in Utah, again with Kanab and its near-by ruins as my first objective. After a day-long ride from Salt Lake City, our train, a mixed-freight, finally reached its destination at Marysvale, in Piute County, a little later than usual because the engineer had stopped twice so that he and the conductor could shoot quail. Dinners along the way and lodging at the hotel had to be ordered in advance by railroad telegraph. The brakeman took these reservations, not by name but by number—seventeen for dinner and five for the night. I found the hotel a two-story, unpainted structure with at least two double beds per room and bolsters instead of pillows.

Next morning, space with the mailman being pre-empted, I bought a ride with a telephone repairman as far as Panguitch, then a drowsy little tree-shaded Mormon town but since grown into a tourist center. It was in Panguitch, after a very satisfying lunch at a roadside diner, that I left three nickels for the waitress only to have them flung after me with a very positive "I'll have you know I'm a good girl."

My reasoning that if I could get to Panguitch I could get farther proved correct. With five men, including the local sheriff and a young horse thief, we left Panguitch in a second Ford at 2:00 P. M. and, a few miles beyond, transferred to still another. This latter was owned by the sheriff from Kanab and driven by his daughter, a tall, thin woman who leaned forward close over the wheel. Since the sheriff and his prisoner occupied the rear seat, I sat with the daughter, and because the car had no brakes it was my job to control speed by pulling

72

up from time to time on a sapling wired to the running board. Incredible though it seems, we reached Kanab safely about 8:30 that night, 140 miles and fourteen hours from my starting point. Ten miles an hour was considered very good time. But what really rankled was to have some young whipper-snapper in the comptroller's office back in Washington deny my expense account because I had not used the interurban. So far as I am aware, there was at that time no interurban west of the Mississippi, a fact apparently unknown to the Washingtonian.

My sights had been set on the little-known region north of the Grand Canyon—the region that had tempted me repeatedly. But all reports agreed: water pockets were dry and forage short. A pack-horse trip in early summer was inadvisable. Why not wait for next winter and meanwhile work the ruins closer at hand? There were caves to explore in Johnson Canyon, a few miles to the east and pottery-strewn mounds near at hand. In this dilemma I turned for advice to B. A. Riggs, one of the original settlers, on whom I had previously leaned. "Old Brig," as he was known to young and old in Kanab, promptly issued an invitation for me to investigate ruins on his ranch some ten miles to the north.

Headquarters for the Riggs ranch were located in Cottonwood Canyon, and it was a devious ride to get there. Our road passed several flooded caves in Lake Canyon, and we splashed through hub-deep water to reach our destination. There the cabin door was thrown wide open and I was told to feel at home. The boys would do the cooking; "Old Brig" and I would look around. Several small groups of one-story dwellings occupied shallow caves below the ranch house, each identified in my notes by distance and direction from "the orchard." White-faced cattle ranged the cedar-covered mesas, but the house and its water supply were fenced. Appearances suggested that ladies of the family lived here from time to time.

Brigham Riggs was never an old man even though he looked to be one; he was called "Old Brig" to distinguish him from a son of the same name. He stood about six feet three inches tall and weighed approximately 160 pounds. He wore a rusty-brown beard down to the fifth button and could sit on his boot heels for hours without twitching. His lean arms had the strength of a Ford spring. He told me much of local history and, then and later, always had something worth while to suggest if weather or finances prevented fulfillment of my schedule. Being a good Mormon, he neither swore, smoked, nor drank. When I suggested future studies north of the Grand Canyon, he introduced the men in charge of the Kaibab National Forest and recommended as prospective guides "Uncle Jim" Owens and Jack Weston, official mountain-lion hunters.

James T. Owens was a professional hunter. He maintained a camp on the Kaibab Forest for himself, his helpers, and a pack of hounds but for no one else. He had guided President Theodore Roosevelt and party over the Kaibab on a lion hunt, yet he professed to know nothing of Indian ruins. And he did not want to guide me. But Jack Weston did, and he and his dogs were just starting out on a periodic cougar hunt. Jack usually traveled alone, for which reason his mule-drawn conveyance sagged to one side. After the dogs accepted me as a member of the party, we got on famously. My bedroll was thrown on behind. Where the buggy could not go, we continued with pack mules. Together we explored the dark corners of Saddle Canyon, Tater Canyon, North Canyon, and South Canyon and eventually drew rein at Cane Springs, headquarters of the Grand Canyon Cattle Company, for a dinner of canned corn and peas with the cowboys.

74

Always, when I was their guest, cowboys ate nothing but canned peas and corn, or so it seemed.

On our way from Kanab to Jacob Lake and House Rock Valley, jogging across the sandy wastes bordering Snake Gulch and up the stepped approach to Kaibab Plateau—we had already told each other all there was to tell—Jack fell to speculating upon the outfit that had preceded us and left its mark upon the road we followed. Every half-mile or so brought an observation of knowledgeable interest—the wide tracks were those of a hayrake whose left wheel was bent at the axle; the motive power was an unshod brown horse (a hoofprint and piece of hide on a slippery rock furnished this clue); the thills were cottonwood saplings, etc., etc. And, sure enough, we pulled in at Old House Rock corrals just minutes behind the outfit which Jack had tracked all the way from Fredonia. It was a sad combination and its fate predictable: an old man and a broken-down horse; the tine-less axle of a discarded hayrake; two aspen poles for shafts with miscellaneous boards nailed to their butt ends as a sort of platform; a paper suitcase, a bedroll, and a box of edibles wired to the platform. The proprietor of this contrivance expected to cross the Colorado at Lees Ferry and prospect for minerals in the San Francisco Mountains, a hundred miles away. At least that is what he said. He would not believe that Lees Ferry had been abandoned ten years before our chance meeting beside the trail.

The ferry site, at the mouth of the Paria, was pre-empted about 1870 by John Doyle Lee, a Mormon fanatic, in an effort to avoid arrest for his part in the Mountain Meadows massacre. He called his cottonwood-shaded retreat "Lonely Dell," surely an honest appellation. Lee was executed in 1877, twenty years after the massacre, but his ferry was operated intermittently thereafter by a succession of owners

75

until 1929 when the Grand Canyon, or "Lees Ferry," bridge was opened for travel.

Most prospectors in my experience were stubborn men. There was the disbeliever whom we met at Bluff City in 1907, his mind fixed on gold fields where a government map showed nothing but smooth walking. And there was the Scandinavian lumberjack who helped with restoration of Betatakin Ruin in 1917 until he tired of Arizona snowstorms and decided to walk to Monticello, Utah—150 miles distant by Indian trail and road—there to prospect in the Blue Mountains. And there were the two placer miners who walked up from the San Juan River in 1908 just to see a little civilization at Oljeto. These two were perhaps the last of their kind for others had panned fruitlessly for gold in those same muddy waters and the timbers of broken dredges rotted along the shore or in midstream.

House Rock Valley, where we left the old prospector and his improvised conveyance, was controlled at the time by the Grand Canyon Cattle Company. Cowboys kept watch from Old House Rock corrals and from New House Rock, more familiarly known as "Cane Springs." Thousands of whitefaces roamed the broad valley, and a small herd of buffalo grazed the southern half. Experimentally or otherwise, crosses between the two were locally called "cattalo"; but, although heavier, they apparently never became commercially profitable. Highway 89 now crosses the Río Colorado five or six miles below Lees Ferry and, with scarcely a thought for the cattle, the buffalo, or the cattalo, hurries through House Rock Valley and on to the physical comforts of modern inns and lodges in the Kaibab Forest.

All this modernization, with silver and linen on the tables, has come about since I rode the Kaibab. There were no accommodations for tourists at that time. One camped any-

76

where and bathed and washed one's clothing in roadside pools, if at all. Jacob Lake was a ranger station; its unlocked cabin and corrals were open for any man and his mount in need of shelter. Deer roamed the forest glades without fear, and mountain lions were occasionally seen in broad daylight. Despite its chattering squirrels, the Kaibab was a quiet and peaceful place.

When we camped near the summit one night, my guide told an after-supper story that sounds plausible but may not be entirely true. A new restaurant had just opened on the North Rim and three of the House Rock cowboys, tired of the same camp food day after day, decided to ride up and give it a trial. And that is what they told the waitress as she passed a lengthy menu to each. "We've been eating canned peas and canned corn so long we thought we'd come up and have ourselves a real blowout." The first one studied the unfamiliar items listed on his card and finally said, "Bring me a plate of baked beans." Meanwhile the second cowboy, running his eyes up and down the card, reached his own decision: "Bring me a plate of baked beans and a bottle of catsup." The third rider gave up without a struggle; he, too, ordered baked beans. At which the waitress turned toward the kitchen as she remarked, "Well, you boys certainly are planning a blowout."

Westward from Lees Ferry the Vermilion Cliffs wall House Rock Valley on the north, and beyond them lies the fantastic Paria Plateau. The south margin of the Paria is bordered by cedars and piñons, and from this green fringe the sandy surface slopes away gently to the north and there ends abruptly at Buckskin Gulch, thirty feet wide and three hundred feet deep. Aboriginal steps lead down into the gorge, but I had no urge to follow them.

During a postwar revisit to the Kanab area in 1920, I spent

77

parts of two days on the Paria hunting prehistoric house sites, but an even greater attraction was the local water supply. This had been developed by Joe Hamblin, a weather-worn son of the famous Mormon missionary, Jacob Hamblin. Rainwater falling on a vast expanse of bare sandstone was funneled into a pile of wind-blown sand below the cliff. Pipes carried the water from this natural reservoir to concrete tanks, and, lacking any other source, Hamblin's cattle trailed in to water of their own accord, thus reducing control to a minimum. A grizzled veteran of wind and sun, our host wore a perpetual squint as protection, I soon came to know, from the blinding glare of unfiltered sunlight on incredibly white sand. It was the whitest sand I ever crossed on horseback. Only a pair of Eskimo-like goggles, fashioned from cardboard, dimmed its reflected brightness.

Jacob Hamblin was a man whom I should have liked to know despite all the harsh words said about him. He was a pathfinder, a trail blazer. He had an uncommon ability to get along with Indians, all Indians, an accomplishment that accounts for the fact that he was repeatedly chosen as Brigham Young's emissary on exploratory journeys on both sides of the Colorado River. With eleven companions Jacob Hamblin was sent in 1858 as the first Mormon missionary to the Hopi villages. In 1873 he marked a wagon route from Lees Ferry to the San Francisco Mountains and later led several companies of colonists along that road to found new settlements throughout central Arizona.

Jacob Hamblin is credited, at least in Kanab, with having guided and counseled Major John Wesley Powell in the latter's conquest of the Grand Canyon in 1869 and 1870, and young Joe Hamblin lent a helping hand. It is said, also, that Joe later assisted C. D. Walcott and W. H. Holmes in their mapping of the country north of the Grand Canyon under the

78

direction of Professor A. H. Thompson of the U.S. Geological Survey. Ben Hamblin, his family connections undetermined, is said to have accompanied the Mindeleff brothers in their survey of Canyon de Chelly and Zuñi pueblo in the middle 1880's. The Mindeleffs were from the Bureau of Ethnology, a unit of the Smithsonian, and because of my association with both institutions Joe and his nephew invited me to share a modest meal with them at their cow camp on the Paria.

Its name alone, Bright Angel Creek, was enough to urge a 1920 side trip. Rumor of rarely seen cliff dwellings deep within the gorge was a further inducement. Dave Rust of Kanab said he knew the place, close under the Walhalla Plateau, and would take me there for ten dollars a day. But the "creek" was too high with melted snow water and too wild for safety. It poured from a huge ten-foot hole high under the rimrock, like water gushing from a hose. After three crossings, at one of which I was humiliatingly unseated, we tied the horses and walked to the Ribbon Falls ruins. Rough water barred further advance, and we did not attempt to reach the mouth of the canyon where Major Powell camped on August 15, 1869, and where he coined the name "Bright Angel" to contrast its clear white water with the muddy flood of "the Dirty Devil," farther upriver. Here, at the mouth of the Bright Angel, the Fred Harvey people have since built their secluded retreat, "Phantom Ranch," a retreat where I have repeatedly promised myself a vacation.

Beaver Creek, flowing into Bright Angel from the east, had been thoroughly trapped long ago, but at least one beaver survived in 1920, for we saw a recently repaired dam. Piute Indians who formerly lived there while gathering and roasting cactus fruits—their "yant" pits are numerous—may have exterminated the beavers, but I never learned why the National Park Service, in its wisdom, should have renamed that green tributary "Wall Creek."

From a night camp at the head of Bright Angel we looked out across Grand Canyon to the sparkling lights of El Tovar, at least fifteen miles away, and watched the headlight of the evening train from Williams as it crept nearer and nearer and finally stopped and blinked out. The night was clear and crisp and the stars hung almost within arm's reach. It was a night for sleeping under the pines, but our mules were nervous at their tether and repeatedly snorted warnings as they stared into the darkness. "Mules make mighty good watchdogs, alert to every strange sound," said my guide. He finally got up to investigate and found fresh cougar tracks. He put another log on the fire and returned to his blankets. Mountain lions, he stated, have a preference for horse and mule flesh—a timely bit of information, to be sure, with mules and horses our only means of transportation.

West of Paria Plateau and west of Kanab are two colorful areas, Zion Canyon and Bryce Canyon, which local residents urged me to see but which I, as a federal employee, felt lay outside my official instructions. Both areas are now national parks, and I may go down in history as the only individual who knowingly let government orders take precedence over personal privilege. The glories of Bryce and Zion still await the favorable future.

Those were the days of long journeys and short appropriations. Four separate times I went to Kanab: the first, as previously explained, on a quick survey of unmapped Antelope Valley; later, with hope of penetrating the barren area between the Utah line and the Grand Canyon. Twice I failed in this latter venture because scant winter snows had left water pockets dry. Success crowned my third effort when a youth whose name I have forgotten took me to Mount Trumbull and back in a wired-together Model T with a water barrel roped to the rear deck. The cost, unfortunately, had to come out of my own pocket.

Mount Trumbull was the end of our road. A cluster of empty pens and shearing sheds told us that the spring clip had been harvested and the sheep moved to greener grazing. Beyond the sheds we followed the uncertain trail of a herder's wagon to the lower Toroweap Valley. From there, just because we wanted to see what lay beyond, we walked to the rim of the Grand Canyon and spent an idle moment looking down into that bottomless gorge with its ever changing patterns of sunlight and shadow.

North or northeast of the shearing pens a basalt surface layer several feet thick had slumped to leave a conspicuous depression a hundred feet in diameter, more or less. My driver called it a "pothole," and on the far side settling of the rock had created a cavelike recess where Indians had found temporary shelter at some time and had left one or more burials. The cave had been thoroughly ransacked for curios, but we noted fragments of yucca sandals among the rubbish and scattered human bones. Those sandal fragments differed in no wise from others I had seen in cliff-dwellings east of the Colorado, but I would not venture to guess their age. Why any Indian, prehistoric or modern, should have wandered out into this empty country except to hunt antelope was another question for which I had no answer.

A decade after this last adventure, chance took me to southern Arizona on a hurry-up assignment. The Bureau of Indian Affairs was about to clear fifty thousand acres of prospective cotton land on the Pima Indian Reservation bordering the Gila River. Contracts had been let; men and machines were already at work. Heavy steel rails drawn by tractors were scraping away every bush and shrub. Bulldozers stood

81

ready to level hillocks and abandoned irrigation canals. That same Pima land was contoured by former irrigation "ditches" or canals, each of which led upriver to an abandoned intake. Some of those canals may have been in use when Father Eusebio Kino first came this way, in 1692; some may have been older.

In large part, Arizona history is based upon irrigation agriculture. Both the Gila and the Salt rivers furnished water for aboriginal irrigation long before white men arrived to usurp Indian lands. The Pimas and Papagos and their ancestors, the Hohokams, were all experienced irrigationists.

Senator Carl Hayden, desirous of saving a record of former canals on that portion of the Pima Reservation then being cleared, appealed to the Smithsonian Institution and the U. S. Army for co-operation. An aerial survey was suggested as the easiest means of recovering the desired data in the emergency. Accordingly the army ordered Lieutenant Edwin Bobzien and Sergeant R. A. Stockwell to fly in from Crissy Field, San Francisco, and photograph the entire canal network from the air, and the Smithsonian sent me along to give them guidance.

In January, 1929, we soon learned that early morning or late afternoon offered the most favorable time for photography since a low sun cast long shadows that brought canal banks into relief. But early morning and late afternoon also brought a ground haze or smoke blanket that tended to obscure the features we were charged to record. Our principal frustration, however, was owing to the fact that all abandoned canals looked exactly alike from an elevation of five thousand feet. We could not distinguish a twenty-year-old ditch from one dug two hundred years earlier.

Some of those Gila River canals, like those bordering the Salt River, were undoubtedly of prehistoric origin; some were known to be the product of men still living. In 1879, Mormon pioneers settling upon the area about Mesa, east of Phoenix, cleared and utilized portions of prehistoric irrigation "ditches" in their own farming—ditches that were still in use at the time of our survey. Those pioneers organized and were followed by a succession of irrigation companies, each of which made its own survey and dug its own canals. But, old or older, those water courses all led upriver to intakes that, of necessity, were rebuilt or replaced as the river annually deepened its channel. Those man-made canals totaled several hundred miles, but it was absolutely impossible to distinguish the oldest from the latest.

In consequence of what we saw from the air, I recommended that plotting of the prehistoric canal networks along both the Gila and Salt rivers be accompanied by close study of all maps prepared by the various post-1878 canal companies and still available. That seemed a necessary preliminary. However, the funds required for such a study were never forthcoming. About 1955, the harvest of Sergeant Stockwell's capable camera was transferred to the University of Arizona for their researches in arid-land agriculture.

A second result of our aerial survey was a lasting friendship with two worth-while Arizona citizens: Odd S. Halseth and L. C. Boies. Both were much interested in our project and went out of their way to expedite it. Halseth, a Norwegian sailor, had left his ship in San Francisco to enlist in the Air Corps at the beginning of World War I; in 1930, a recognized authority on prehistoric Arizona canals, he presided over the city's "Park of Four Waters" at Phoenix, with its museum, remnants of four ancient irrigation canals, and ruins of a contemporary adobe structure called "Pueblo Grande."

Like Halseth, "Cal" Boies was a veteran of 1917 but, far

from the sea, he was raising cattle in Arizona when the call came for volunteers. The partner whom he left in charge of their combined herd and the ranch buildings sold the entire outfit during the war and disappeared. True soldier that he was, Boies came home with empty pockets, picked up a job selling autos, and later, while our aerial survey was under way, enlivened each evening with his guitar and a choice selection of old trail songs that matched his rich baritone. Eventually he was elected county sheriff, an office to which he was repeatedly returned by his fellow citizens.

It was in his capacity as county sheriff that Cal Boies, still a bit bowlegged from cowboy days but complete master of his domain, paved my way among dwellers of the rugged Nantack Mountains in 1931, when I was sent out in search of alleged prehistoric baskets. He knew everyone, good and bad, in the Nantack country, and they knew him.

The "prehistoric" baskets someone had seen in a half-hidden cave and so reported to the Smithsonian proved to be of Apache manufacture—possibly left there in the 1880's by Geronimo or one of his warrior bands. I shipped them back to Washington nonetheless and gained a renewed admiration for men who could bake Dutch-oven bread with a few cottonwood twigs and serve rich black coffee from an old tomato can that had been scoured with sand and a bit of burlap. The fact is not generally known today, but statistics prove that some of the best coffee ever brewed was made in a discarded can picked up beside the trail.

V

BETATAKIN AND THE CLAY HILLS

IN 1916, CONGRESS AUTHORIZED an Interior Department
appropriation of $3,000 to cover the preservation and repair,
under supervision of the Smithsonian Institution, of prehistoric ruins in Navaho National Monument, Arizona. Early
in March, 1917, I was unexpectedly named to represent the
Institution on this joint undertaking, and, because Interior
Department funds were involved, I was sworn in as a dis-
bursing agent of the Bureau of Indian Affairs, a prominent
unit of Interior.

While receiving instructions and advice from a Bureau
representative who had never been west of the Alleghenies,
I was also informed of the diversity of reports which I was expected to submit during field work. There were daily reports,
weekly reports, monthly reports, and bimonthly reports. Each
had its own designated color, with a specified number of
carbon copies; each was to be neatly typed, double space.
Midway of these instructions I interrupted to say that a single
report upon conclusion of my assignment would have to
suffice. And it did.

I boarded a train at Washington, D.C., on March 16, 1917
(unexpended funds had to be returned to the Treasury by
June 30, the end of the fiscal year). I reached Flagstaff,
Arizona, three days later, hired five chance laborers from
a street corner, and left with them on the twentieth by automobile for Tuba City, seventy-five miles distant, western
agency for the Bureau of Indian Affairs. Sheltered from win-

try winds by the old octagonal trading post at Tuba, we transferred to John Wetherill's four-horse freight wagon, driven by his faithful Navaho teamster, Chischili-begay. From Tuba it was seventy-five or eighty miles to the Wetherill trading post at Kayenta with two nights in the open on snow-covered ground, and from Kayenta by saddle horse and pack mule another fifteen or twenty miles to Betatakin, our first objective. Thus, within a week, I utilized four means of transportation—the best the country offered—to reach my destination.

Chischili-begay was a long-haired Navaho who spoke no English. If he understood what was wanted, he never asked questions. He did what had to be done. About 1907, when a Ute raiding party attacked the Wetherill-Colville trading post at Oljeto, Chischili-begay was sent for help, and, riding through Monument Valley at a gallop, he was shot at by one of the Utes. The ball missed its mark but broke the pommel of his saddle. As late as 1923, that broken saddle still hung in Wetherill's store.

Although the Congressional appropriation clearly anticipated repair and preservation of all three major ruins on the Monument, I knew that such an undertaking was utterly impossible within our allotted time. Thus I resolved to restrict our efforts to Betatakin because it was most accessible to tourists and, for this very reason, perhaps in greatest need of early stabilization. All three ruins were responsibilities of the National Park Service, but there was no Service man present in 1917.

Betatakin ("Hillside House" in Navaho) had been discovered in early July, 1909, by Professor Byron Cummings, then of the University of Utah, and I was one of his student assistants. The date was July 5, as I recall, or a day or two either way. Professor Cummings and his party were returning

The middle portion of Betatakin Ruin, 1917.

A modern reproduction of an ancient Betatakin ladder.

The middle portion of Betatakin Ruin, Navaho National Monument, Arizona, in 1917, before excavation.

The pecked notches that provided wall-supports at Betatakin,
1917.

Jack Martin watering his horses during the National Geographic Society's reconnaissance of the Chaco Canyon country, 1920. On the wagon, left to right, are Charles Martin, National Geographic Society photographer; Earl H. Morris, American Museum of Natural History; Sylvanus G. Morley, Carnegie Institution of Washington.

Joe Hamblin, son of the famous Mormon missionary Jacob
Hamblin, at his cattle ranch on Paria Plateau, southern Utah,
in 1920.

On the old Piute trail, west side of Grand Gulch, Utah, in 1923.

Graham Canyon, an eastern tributary of Grand Gulch, in 1923.

Pueblo Bonito, New Mexico, at the end of the 1924 season.

Hoski Yazie and Dan Dubois, enemies of former days and still wary of each other, at the dedication of the Fred Harvey Hotel, "El Navaho," Gallup, New Mexico, on May 25, 1923.

The Wetherill-Colville trading post at Kayenta, Arizona, in 1923.
The Wetherill home is at right rear.

A Navaho grandmother, shaded from the midday sun, rides forth to make a social call. Photographed west of Crownpoint, New Mexico, in 1925.

"The Zuñi woman" in 1926. She had lived among the Navahos
all her life.

"Black Bottom," a daily visitor to the National Geographic Society Pueblo Bonito camp, in 1927. His Navaho mother took pride in creating assorted necklaces for him, but left his rear side unadorned.

Don Lorenzo Hubbell and his son, Román, at the old Hubbell
home at Ganado, Arizona, in 1929.

A 1924 gift to the Macaw clan at Zuñi. This bird, photographed
in 1939, feathered many prayer plumes before it died.

from explorations in upper Segi Canyon when his chief guide and interpreter, John Wetherill, stopped to chat with a Navaho family beside the trail and, incidentally, to inquire about any near-by ruins. The Segi and its branches were all new to John Wetherill in 1909; it was his first trip through the canyon.

The woman of the household (Navahos are matrilineal) described a large cave dwelling in a gorge across the way, and one of the men agreed to lead us to it. Dean Cummings paid five dollars for this service, but the Navaho, typical of his kind, advanced only part way, then indicated direction by thrusting out his chin and sat down beside the trail to await return of the others. As a Navaho he would have nothing to do with the Anasazis, "the ancient ones," and dared not enter a ruin for fear of the "chindies," ghosts of the ancient people.[1]

Our examination at that time was very superficial, for Wetherill was in a hurry to return to his home at Oljeto whence he was to leave next day on a business trip to Gallup. Also, being on sabbatical leave from the university, Professor Cummings expected to return in the fall to examine the ruin more minutely. During our hurried tour we found a stone pipe on a bench in one of the ceremonial rooms, a couple of fragments of basketry, and numerous potsherds. Potsherds were everywhere, hundreds of them.

Betatakin occupies a high-vaulted cave at the end of a box canyon, an unnamed south branch of the main Segi. Cliffs of reddish-brown Navaho sandstone arch above the ruin and wall the canyon. "Navaho," a geological designation for a variety of sedimentary sandstone, was singularly appropriate in this instance since we were in Navaho country

[1] John Wetherill, Southwestern National Monument Monthly Bulletin, Supp. P. A. (June, 1934); *The Plateau*, Vol. XXVII, No. 4 (April, 1955).

and all our neighbors were Navahos. On the occasion of that 1909 visit I naturally had no thought that eight years later I would be back again, to assist the Interior Department in preserving Betatakin for the future.

At an elevation of seven thousand feet the Betatakin area is no warm resort, especially in early spring. In March, 1917, we broke trail through two feet of snow to establish camp among scrub oaks below the ruin, the flattest bit of ground anywhere around. Since there was no forage for our saddle animals we sent them back to Kayenta, leaving ourselves isolated and afoot. Not anticipating so much winter, I had come unprepared and had to borrow tents from Wetherill and Colville. The tents were of lightweight canvas; the ground, wet and cold. A raised hearth lifted coffeepot and Dutch oven above the snow, but only the great ruin and its empty rooms provided shelter when the wind blew and ice formed on the canyon stream.

Initially, in 1917, we tested the talus slope for burials, then cleared away tons of blown sand that had settled below a mid-cave seepage zone. A band of columbine greened the upper part of this seepage; in the lower half, a thicket of scrub oaks had taken root, covering the wreckage of shattered walls. In its prime, Betatakin consisted of perhaps 150 rooms or more. From the number of families those rooms represented, there should have been several deaths each generation; but, as at other major Navaho Monument ruins, we found no discoverable burial place either in the talus or about the dwellings.

During clearing operations we happened upon a former village spring and readied it for use again. Broken timbers and building stones suitable for repairs were piled to one side. When it was noticed that some of the ancient mortar had outlasted the sandstone blocks it bound together, we began experimenting with different proportions of sand, clay, and rock. Eventually we were able to duplicate that ancient mortar and thereafter employed it with great satisfaction in all our repair work and rebuilding of walls.

Betatakin fills a broad, southward-facing cave. Its Navaho name, "Hillside House," was well chosen for, except at its two extremes, the cave floor has a slope of approximately forty-five degrees, thus requiring seatings to support house walls built upon it. To meet this requirement the ancient builders pecked with stone hammers a succession of shallow cups, lateral depressions the size and depth of an oyster shell. Half a dozen were needed for the average wall. These hand-pecked seatings are a distinct feature of every Navaho National Monument ruin with which I am acquainted, for every cave in that particular region has a downward- and forward-sloping floor. Only by providing basal supports could the builders erect a stone-and-mud wall on such a slope.

Stonework for front walls normally rose three to five feet above their seatings, to floor level of the room under construction. Very often the outer end of that room consisted of wickerwork—wattled willows plastered inside and out with mud. However inadequate wickerwork may seem to us, it obviously answered the purpose since it is to be found everywhere. Side walls, whether of wickerwork or masonry, invariably stood upon a series of notches rising with the slope. Thus, in all our repairs we were at pains to provide suitable seatings for walls, both at the end of a room and at its side. And all our seatings, cut with steel chisels, purposely exceeded in depth what would have satisfied the ancient masons.

In late April messengers brought news of United States entry into World War I, and a few days later an Indian policeman from the Bureau agency in Tuba City appeared with papers from a too-zealous local draft board informing the six of us—the only strangers in Navaho County—that we had all been selected for the armed services. A foot-loose Indian who had become a regular weekend visitor at our camp was curious to know what all this war talk was about. When he asked who the Germans were and why Washington was going to fight them, I did my best to oblige; with an inadequate knowledge of his language I managed to get the idea across. I told him that from Betatakin by saddle horse it was two days' ride to Shiprock, then three or four days to Santa Fe. From Santa Fe it would take a good rider twenty-five or thirty days to reach New York and, from there, a whole week in a big boat to get across the big water. After that, about three more days of riding to get to where the Americans and Germans were fighting.

After studying this prospect for a moment or two our guest replied: "You tell Washington the Germans never did anything to us Navahos and we are not mad at them, but if Washington wants to fight the Mexicans we will all go."

Our weekend visitor was a handsome young Navaho with a good horse and a wandering habit. Also he was something of a dandy, dressed in cotton pants with an outside split to the knee, a red velvet jacket with silver conchas, necklace and numerous bracelets, and hair tied up in a bun at the nape of his neck. A Pendleton blanket over his shoulder was coat or bed as necessity required. Apparently he liked our company for on one occasion he brought along a huge white tent, fully ten by fourteen feet, and pitched it on the levelest space available, close to our outdoor kitchen. Although reasonably flat, the space nevertheless had a slope that left a ten-inch gap under the front end. When the owner was absent this tent was absolutely empty, but he had the foresight always to tie a keyless padlock on the paired straps that bound flaps together. Obviously he had many friends or relatives in the vicinity for he was always on the go and rarely spent more than a night or two with us.

My most loyal and indispensable helper during these Betatakin restorations was another Navaho, perhaps in his early twenties, who wore his long hair tied in the traditional bun with a length of woolen cord. We knew him as "Sharkey's Boy." He spoke no English but was a willing worker, keenly interested in what we were doing and with the ability to anticipate what was required. He was perhaps the strongest man I ever knew. When it came time to install ladders connecting the various courts, I had only to show him the individual problem and he would trot off with an ax on his shoulder and in due time return with the trunk of a cedar tree, the wood green and a foot or more in diameter, and of a weight I could not estimate.

The tree trunk in its corner, Sharkey would trim its branches to proper length and cut notched steps at suitable intervals. Also he quickly learned how to imitate a prehistoric ladder, its rundles lashed in place with yucca strips; how to weave a wattled wall and how to make a ceiling, cedar bark over willows and mud on top. Our restoration of Betatakin—and I understand it has proved eminently successful—is owing in large measure to the intelligence and interest of a long-haired Navaho, "Sharkey's Boy."

At the east and west ends of the village the cave floor flattened out, and here open areas were walled at cliff edge to form outdoor rooms or courts for leisurely household activities and neighborhood gossip. In neither case, apparently, was the court wall ever more than a foot or two high. The west-end court, Number 10 on my published ground plan, also supported a long, thin pine pole that extended up thirty or thirty-five feet to a shallow ledge faced by a gallery wall. That ledge wall, only two or three feet high, was un-

91

broken by openings of any sort. I never learned what lies behind it.

Other open workrooms or courts were spaced haphazardly about the pueblo. Pecked steps leading up the slanting cave floor, through these courts and under adjoining rooms, show that Betatakin had expanded east and west as the local population increased in number and required more shelter. Although timbers for roof construction were readily available, we noted several instances in which beams had been spliced and bound together with strips of yucca leaves. Ceiling poles sometimes were placed butt to tip as though to equalize floor thickness. Lateral doors and especially those leading to storage places were ordinarily fitted with stone slabs set in grooved jambs. Pliable loops and wedges on each side probably held the slabs in place. Roof hatchways naturally required no such fastening device.

On house walls and occasionally on the cliff above and back of the village, broad and narrow grooves showed where stone axes and bone awls had been sharpened. Cut into the floor of Room 39 were four cylindrical loom anchors, each about three inches in depth and provided with a transverse stick that fitted into a spiraled groove. Paired eyelets pecked to meet below the surface of a projecting cliff edge are believed to have been supporting anchors for a waist loom—one that hung from above and was held taut by weight of the weaver.

In all our restorations at Betatakin we endeavored to preserve the aboriginal atmosphere of the place by duplicating as nearly as possible the handiwork of the ancient builders. For wattled walls—and there were many—we bound willow shoots vertically to horizontal members by means of yucca strips and plastered the whole with mud, inside and out.

Being farmers primarily, residents of Betatakin sometimes

92

went as hungry as we did during restoration of their terraced cave village. Food was hard to come by in the Kayenta area in March and April, 1917. The Navahos had sold their last wool clip for 35 cents a pound and did not want to work. High prices made them independent. The road to Gallup was long, cold, and muddy; the wet-weather freight rate of $2.50 a hundred tempted no one. Wetherill's household supplies were nearly exhausted, but these were generously shared with us, including dehydrated vegetables left by some citified explorer.

For days at a time we in camp had nothing to eat but rice. When coffee gave out, we made a brew of "Brigham's tea," a low leafless plant with jointed stems which I first came to know over in western Utah. Because we could not keep a horse at the ruin on account of the snow, I walked to Kayenta three separate times to beg foodstuffs, anything available. I happened to be there one day when twenty pack burros arrived with flour from Farmington, New Mexico, and saw it sold immediately at ten cents a pound. The Navahos had to have their wheat-flour bread irrespective of weather and roads. Life in Navaho-land has always been on a catch-as-catch-can basis, but never more so than in the spring of 1917.

In early June at the end of our Betatakin work, four of us begged a ride to Flagstaff with the Kayenta schoolmaster, a stocky and personable individual unseasonably attired in a black derby hat and a black winter suit. It was a day-long trip, but we were prepared for it: oil, gas, and water containers were freshly filled and strapped to one running board, bedrolls were roped to the other, and canvas water bags dangled from an extra tire at the rear. Along about Red Lake drifted sand proved too much for narrow tires so we let out the air to ride on top. Then inner tubes had to be patched

93

and the tires pumped up again. A mile or so down the road we wrapped our bedroll ropes around the tires, then spread the canvas tarps upon the sand for surer traction. By the time we reached Tuba City our overweight host had lost several pounds, and his white silk cravat was wet and clinging. But his Model T saved the day; we did not have to walk. As a labor-saving device those early Fords had no equal!

Five years later or thereabouts, my long-time friend, A. V. Kidder, upon completing excavations at historic Pecos pueblo southeast of Santa Fe, motored all over the Southwest in a well-traveled but faithful Ford he called "Old Blue." Its original floorboards had long since gone for fuel, but where Kidder wanted to go Old Blue found a way.

Perhaps equally well known throughout northern Arizona and northwestern New Mexico at that time were Earl H. Morris and "Old Black." Far out among the Lukachukai Mountains one day the dry sand proved too much, and Old Black burned out a bearing. Morris contemplated his predicament overnight and then replaced the bearing with a square of bacon rind and so finished out the season. You don't get bacon rind like that any more!

Model T's were everywhere in the 1920's. Kidder's "Old Blue" and Earl Morris's "Old Black" were only two of a long and faithful lineage. Like Navaho sheep they stood well off the ground; they were designed to straddle high centers, to go where any other four-legged creature could go. From the time they got their first wagons at Fort Defiance and elsewhere after Bosque Redondo, Navaho men drove those wagons on trails which they had formerly ridden horseback. After Model T's replaced wagons, the same old horse trails were traveled by Model T's—until the gas gave out. Long-haired Navahos never fed their horses and rarely bought more than one gallon of gas at a time.

94

Late summer, 1923, found me back in Kayenta once more. The National Geographic Society had asked me to have a look at the Clay Hills country, west of Grand Gulch in southeastern Utah, and I had turned first of all to John Wetherill as a prospective guide. He had participated in the exploitation of Grand Gulch in the 1890's, and thus knew at least the eastern fringe of the country I was to examine.

More to the point, I had a deep admiration for John Wetherill. I had known him at Oljeto in 1908 and 1909, when northern Arizona was young and the Navahos were wild. He had guided the Cummings-Douglass party to discovery of Rainbow Bridge on August 14, 1909; he had been my chief reliance during restoration of Betatakin for the Interior Department in the late winter of 1917. A Quaker by birth and inclination, he could shoe a mule without swearing, and he could lead a pack train where a pack train had never gone before. The Clay Hills country was unmapped and virtually untraveled, but I knew that John Wetherill could take me there if anyone could.

Summer rains fell late in 1923. Motoring over from Pueblo Bonito, my two companions and I had stopped to see the ruins of Canyon de Chelly and so arrived at Kayenta a couple of days later than anticipated. After pushing our sturdy truck mile after muddy mile and building road wherever necessary, we arrived mud spattered and lame. But there was no time for rest. Wetherill had an early commitment with another party, so we rounded up the mules and got under way after a one-night stop.

My original intention had been to follow our Rainbow Bridge trail down Moonlight Creek to its junction with the San Juan River and cross there. But, with the San Juan in flood, we changed plans and took the longer path through Monument Valley to the swinging bridge at Mexican Hat.

95

Aptly named, this cable-hung bridge was something for which our animals were not prepared, and it required a bit of urging to get them across to the north side. Even more than horses, mules resent anything new and unfamiliar. A little dirt scattered on the floor boards made the start look natural, and thereafter, led by Wetherill's horse, the crossing was accomplished without too much protest.

To reduce the number of pack mules and lessen their loads, two Navahos had been hired to meet us at the mouth of the Moonlight with a relief supply of oats three days after our departure from Kayenta. However, as we learned later, they had been diverted to a "squaw dance" and forgot our needs. (It is virtually impossible to keep a Navaho man from a squaw dance.) In this emergency Wetherill swam the flood on a log, walked twenty miles to an oil camp, borrowed a flivver to reach Kayenta, and was back at our river camp in two days.

Two or three days later we came to the Colorado River and turned into Moki Canyon, where progress was slowed—but only momentarily—by quicksand. Quicksand is treacherous and to be avoided, but there was no way of getting around the pool before us with sandstone cliffs on one side, the river on the other. With a whoop and a holler the mules were rushed across the rubbery surface before their small hoofs could cut through, and we were on our way.

John Wetherill was a determined man, especially on the trail. He improvised but never turned back; he always fought his way forward to his intended destination, as with the quicksand at the mouth of Moki Canyon. On another occasion, en route to the discovery of Rainbow Bridge in 1909, he had forgotten the nails needed for reshoeing mules and horses. He had the shoes and shoeing hammer but no nails. Following an accident in lower Copper Canyon, Wetherill salvaged

96

wire nails from an abandoned box to tighten shoes on one of the pack horses. They only lasted halfway up the long Nockai trail, to be sure, but the emergency was met.

That Nockai Canyon trail deserves a special word. It was built by Navahos, and a Navaho never wastes labor. The trail seemed endlessly long as it climbed the precipitous side of Nockai Mesa. Men and horses were thoroughly tired when they reached the top, and there they drank freely, side by side, from shallow pools left by the last passing shower. It mattered to neither man nor beast that those pools were paved with sheep droppings and alive with tiny wigglers. Water is water!

One afternoon in Graham Canyon on the east approach to Grand Gulch, where water, fuel, and grazing for the mules all lay within easy reach, we made an early camp, cooked an early supper, and prepared for a long night. But not John Wetherill! Lolling there on his bedroll, watching the evening shadows climb the canyon walls, he suddenly noticed a small cliff-dwelling high up at the edge of the sunlight and decided to take a look. And I decided to look with him.

It was a stiff climb but rewarding. The cave had not been entered since abandonment; its one-clan kiva was intact, the roof complete and a ladder projecting from its hatchway. Out in front, half-buried in wind-blown sand, a corrugated pot had been placed to catch water dripping from above. Its coils were thickly sooted from ancient fires and its rim partially disintegrated from dampness, but its final non-culinary function was perfectly clear. We scraped out the sand, introduced an initialed stone fragment just to confound some future archaeologist, and refilled the pot.

Making our way up that rocky cliffside, we naturally helped each other as we progressed from ledge to ledge. Wetherill took the lead until, stalled by a six-foot shelf of

97

solid sandstone, he began to squirm and settle his weight down upon my upstretched arms. A coiled rattlesnake was sunning itself on that sandstone ledge.

The kiva, a ceremonial chamber occupying a semi-subterranean position under the cave overhang, was two-thirds full of blown sand, and this was thickly carpeted with cactus dragged in by pack rats. A two-pole ladder with rundles lashed on at suitable intervals thrust itself up through the hatchway. Without a light we could see very little of the interior other than its cribbed ceiling, but the rounded end of a stick thrust between ceiling timbers attracted my attention. Withdrawn, it proved to be a thirty-inch war club of mountain mahogany, its handgrip carved and polished through use. We carried it back to camp and thence to Washington, where it is now preserved in the National Museum.

On a narrow ledge at the back of another cave a small masonry room had been fenced with two horizontal poles as though to guard against a careless step. More interesting, as I recall, was a window-like opening barred by crossed sticks—a feature unique in my experience. I have never seen anything comparable elsewhere; it resembled a window awaiting six glass panes. Near by were the remains of a storage bin made of willows slanted upward and inward to meet the cave roof and thickly plastered with mud—just such bins as I had seen in White Canyon sixteen years before. The middle portion had collapsed but an oval doorway showed at one side, its jambs rounded in a manner reminiscent of granaries constructed by the Basket Makers. But the whole setup, I imagine, was no earlier than Pueblo II— a much later culture horizon as archaeologists measure southwestern history.

Moki Canyon, which I was impatient to see, takes its name from "Moquitch," the Ute word for Hopi. Pueblo III cliff-dwellings occupy caves in the lower part of the canyon and could have inspired the Ute name; earlier remains may be seen in rear recesses of shelters farther to the east. The canyon was never fully occupied, and some of its caves apparently had never been inhabited. But from one of them, a cliff-dwelling "built in a large cave" and thus presumably situated at the lower end of the canyon, a hank of cotton yarn had been found by an unknown traveler about 1890 and sold to an intermediary, from whom it was later acquired by the National Museum.

That cotton yarn, identified as of the distinctive Hopi variety, had long intrigued me as a museum man. It could only represent an import from the Hopi area since Moki Canyon is too far north for successful cotton cultivation. Pueblo priests greatly prized home-grown cotton for some of their ceremonials and would not hesitate to travel long distances to obtain it. But we never identified the ruin from which that museum specimen came.

Rock slides blocked our passage from time to time, and thickets of scrub oak screened low-lying shelters to which we should have forced a path. From this distance it seems as though I probably missed a great deal of human history in this mysterious gorge where peoples built storied houses in high, inaccessible caves, but there is no going back. Vast accumulations of wind-blown sand had folded down over the south cliff, and one of them, after a long, tedious upward climb, eventually provided our escape. Now, I understand, the waters of Lake Powell have risen to fill the canyon, and boatmen may float to the open doorways barred to us in 1923.

Beyond the north rim of Moki Canyon lay a broad waste of bare sandstone, carved by wind, sand, and the runoff of passing showers. Here and there a tuft of grass or a small bush had found root. A few shallow caves were seen at the

99

rounded ends of bowl-shaped, rock-walled valleys. These caves were most easily entered, as I learned from my Navaho companion, by running down across the concave sandstone at a speed countering centripetal force—like a bicycle rider on a banked track. I made a hurried search of two such caves and in one found a bundle of paired twigs, each pair about six inches long and joined by a neat yucca cord with a noose at the end. Later, with the sun lowering, I stopped on a high point to look out to the west beyond the Río Colorado to the Henry Mountains. Named by Major John Wesley Powell in 1869 to honor the secretary of the Smithsonian Institution, Joseph Henry, the Henry Mountains stood there in the misty distance as a sort of bond between my past and present.

That bond was a tenuous one, indeed, for Joseph Henry and Major Powell were former leaders in the institution where I worked from day to day, and their individual achievements are known to relatively few. One of those who remembered was Professor Herbert E. Gregory of Yale and the University of Hawaii. He and I never met on the trail although we became well acquainted as the years progressed. He was in the Oljeto region in 1908, as I was, and was an infrequent caller at the Wetherill-Colville trading post and the modest home Wetherill had built for his wife and children. He climbed Navaho Mountain that year and walked its northern slopes in pursuit of geological knowledge for his famous *Water-Supply Paper 380*, published in 1916.

Gregory was a geologist primarily. Each summer he took time off from teaching to help unravel the mysteries of Southwestern geology for the U.S. Geological Survey. He was especially interested in the Henry Mountains region and repeatedly invited me to join him there, west of the Río Colorado. He planned that together, he as a geologist and I as an archaeologist, would survey that rugged country all the way

100

from the Circle Cliffs to Kaiparowits Plateau, just north of the Paria where my own studies ended. It was a grand idea, but Gregory had to pursue it alone.

In 1923, after leaving Moki Canyon, we traveled a short distance on the old Mormon Trail of 1879 as it climbed rocky ledges from the "Hole-in-the-Rock" crossing of the Río Colorado to Clay Hills Pass and thence around the north end of Grand Gulch to the colonization of Bluff City. For our part we turned south from the Pass on an old Piute trail, swam the San Juan River despite quicksand and the near loss of a pack mule with all our flour, paid a brief remembrance visit to Rainbow Bridge, and hurried on to Kayenta. That was my second trip to the great arch, the first having been as a member of the discovery party fourteen years before, and I was glad to make a "before and after" comparison. John Wetherill, custodian of the monument at the time (his salary was one dollar a year), told me how many had trailed in to see the bridge, but the total failed to stick in my poor memory.

Upon our return to Kayenta after that 1923 trip to the Clay Hills and beyond, the Wetherill home was enlivened by two small Navaho girls, Fanny and Betty, homeless children whom the Wetherills had adopted. The Wetherill-Colville trading post was doing well enough, and there were those who came from a distance to see for themselves the reported marvels of this whole fascinating region. The Wetherill home, its hospitable living room in front and a row of guest quarters at one side, was beginning to anticipate the tourist influx. When I said my farewells to the family, it was without thought of ever seeing Kayenta again.

But, as one of its discoverers, I was invited back to Betatakin in June, 1966, to participate in the dedication of a new office building and a new Visitors' Center for the National

Park Service. All Navahos from roundabout and about two thousand white friends from as far away as Flagstaff were present. Lee Bradley, who had worked for Wetherill and Colville in 1909, my second summer in the area, is now in charge of the Navaho Tribal Park, on the edge of Monument Valley. All else has changed.

Kayenta in 1966 was not as I remembered it. The old trading post had been razed and so, too, most of the old home. John and Louisa Wetherill are buried beside Clyde Colville on the mesa above; their son and daughter are buried elsewhere; Betty and Fanny have homes of their own. The lone day school which I remembered from 1917 has been replaced by District 27 with a resident superintendent, thirty elementary-school teachers, and a dome-shaped high school seating 190 pupils. The long-haired youths whom I saw here in 1909 are now local businessmen or smartly uniformed tribal policemen. And everyone drives a car or, at least, a quarter-ton pickup.

Kayenta today has a permanent non-Indian population of two hundred or more, a post office, a hospital, half a dozen motels each with its curio counter, and restaurants to suit the individual appetite. My companions and I were most hospitably received at the Wetherill Inn Motel, on the hill above the old Wetherill home, and we dined at the new Monument Valley Inn, where State Highway 64 stretches its macadam miles east across Monument Valley to Four Corners and south to Tuba City, Cameron, and famous U.S. Highway 66.

VI

HERE AND THERE

It was at Kayenta that I first met Lorenzo Hubbell, Jr., son and namesake of the revered Don Lorenzo of Ganado. The year was 1917 and I had just ended my stabilization job at Betatakin. "Young Lorenzo," as he was known to everyone across the reservation, left a lasting impression as he turned south in a light buckboard, his 250 pounds inadequately balanced by a small Indian boy beside him. Three years later, in 1920, from his Oraibi trading post he was host to all who attended the Snake Dance at Hotevilla on Third Mesa. Two Hopi women were doing his cooking. As one of his guests on that occasion I sat at the last table, and I still marvel at the amount of free food some of those tourists could eat—baking-powder biscuits, roast lamb and boiled potatoes (and mutton when the lamb was gone), and stewed apricots for dessert.

The Hopi Snake Dance, so called, whether on First Mesa or Third, is a prayer for rain and not a spectacle for the amusement of outsiders as many of these latter assume. Visitors crowded the rooftops, and Indians from far and near ranged themselves along the walls. Knowing that all snakes used in the outdoor ceremony—poisonous and nonpoisonous —were to be released immediately and sent to the four directions with the villagers' plea for rain, my companions and I left for the railroad before the dance ended and before the dance plaza was fully cleared. And none too soon at that. The skies opened and rain came down in torrents; we

103

crossed the Oraibi Arroyo and drove for higher ground with no farewells for our host and his other guests. Ours was a very timely exit. The big, seven-passenger car next behind was caught in the sandy flood and imprisoned there until a tractor came to the rescue. When the Hopis pray for rain, it rains!

Having learned that I intended a 1920 visit to the Hopi pueblos, my genial long-time friend, W. H. Jackson, asked if I would carry a print from one of his 1875 negatives to an acquaintance in Tewa (Hano) on First Mesa. That acquaintance was none other than Nampeyo, and I was delighted to be the messenger. When Jackson took his photograph, Nampeyo (or Num-pa-yu as Jackson wrote the name) was perhaps eighteen or nineteen, her hair done up in side whorls to symbolize the squash-blossom and thus evidence her marriageability. At the time she was keeping house for her brother, chief of the village, and the printed word has since extolled her beauty, her poise, and her gracious hospitality to Jackson and his party. In 1875, Jackson was photographing southwestern Colorado for the Hayden Surveys and had just had a brush with a mixed band of renegade Indians, as previously related, when he decided to cut across northeastern Arizona and have a look at the Hopi towns on their high mesas. It was on this 1875 adventure that he took his memorable picture of Nampeyo.

Twenty years later, when J. W. Fewkes of the Smithsonian was excavating the prehistoric Hopi village of Sikyatki, Nampeyo and her husband, Lesou, daily visited the site to copy the ancient pottery designs on scraps of paper. In consequence of those visits and her successful reproductions of old Sikyatki-ware and its remarkable surface finish, Nampeyo became the most famous of modern Hopi potters; her daughters learned the art from her, and now, I presume, granddaughters are supplying the tourist trade. Formerly these reproductions were to be had at every Fred Harvey curio shop along the Santa Fe, but now they are fewer in number and in greater demand.

In 1920, when I presented Jackson's photograph of forty-five years before, Nampeyo was blind and called upon her granddaughters to describe the offering. She was visibly annoyed, too, when the girls took the print and laughingly directed each other's attention to her bare feet, her old-style woolen dress with the left shoulder exposed, her squash-blossom whorls, her multiple necklaces and turquoise pendants. Nampeyo had been a beauty at eighteen, but her granddaughters were schoolgirls of the present.

At his Oraibi home and trading post, young Lorenzo Hubbell was an echo of his father—a trifle broader and heavier, perhaps, but cast in the same mold and possessed of the same too-generous disposition. A younger son, Román, was managing paternal affairs in 1929 when I stopped overnight at Ganado. Then, as before, Don Lorenzo's home was a low, one-story multiple-roomed adobe house, its screened porch bright with morning-glories. The interior walls were adorned with Navaho blankets, paintings by artists who had been entertained there, books and mementos—a comfortable, unpretentious home from which Spanish-American hospitality had been dispensed for half a century. Indeed, hospitality was finally Don Lorenzo's undoing. His Mexican and American acquaintances were too numerous and some of them simply stayed too long. Because the old Hubbell trading post is the most famous of its period and belongs to an era that will not come again, it was gratifying to this writer to learn in 1966 that the home and store are henceforth to be preserved as a National Historic Site in custody of the National Park Service.

Among Don Lorenzo's Navaho neighbors at Ganado were

105

several veterans of the Kit Carson campaign in 1863 and of Bosque Redondo. One of these elders, whom we may call Hosteen Chee, had been in the habit of coming in periodically with a seamless sack for a contribution of coffee, flour, and other essentials. With edibles provided gratuitously, several of the old man's relatives had moved in with him and brought their several families. They were prepared to stay indefinitely. Finally, Hosteen Chee died and was buried out among the rocks. Two weeks later a son-in-law appeared at the trading post and tossed the seamless sack upon the chest-high counter with a peremptory "Fill 'er up." Don Lorenzo leaned forward across the counter and with gentle finality said, "Hosteen Chee is dead and so is the sack."

C. N. Cotton, a lifelong friend and crony of Lorenzo Hubbell, went west with the building of the Atlantic and Pacific Railroad. A telegraph operator as the rails advanced, he quit the job "along about Guam" in 1882 and became an Indian trader. Whether Don Lorenzo Hubbell influenced this decision I do not know, but the two were in partnership at Ganado in 1884. Ten years later Cotton moved to Gallup, New Mexico, and opened a wholesale business that supplied and financed independent traders in all parts of the reservation. Wetherill and Colville at Oljeto were among his customers in 1908. He was still a wholesale merchant and banker during the years I knew him, 1920 to 1927.

Cotton's warehouse was a conspicuous two-story building west of Main Street and adjoining the Santa Fe tracks, where freight cars loaded and unloaded. His home was a rambling, thick-walled adobe surrounding an open patio where grass grew green and exotic plants stood in tubbed splendor. Choice textiles and trophies from foreign travels adorned the walls, and there were paintings of the West and Southwest by many

106

artists, including Frederic Remington and Charles Russell, and a priceless series of crayon portraits of Hopi men and women by E. A. Burbank.

Sterling silver graced the Cotton table, to which I was repeatedly welcomed, albeit in camp khakis. As a roast leg of lamb on a silver platter was placed before him, my host would remark, knowing the limitations of my customary fare: "I have to eat this stuff every day; you can stand it once in a while."

Like others of his experience, C. N. Cotton was willing to talk about almost anyone except himself. That he had been successful in business was obvious; the cold room in his warehouse was piled ceiling-high with Navaho blankets received in trade, and he predicted that both quality and quantity would decline as Navaho economy increased. In our table-side conversations he told of construction of the Atlantic and Pacific; of transient towns that sprouted along the right of way; of hard-working Chinese tracklayers who were spurned by everyone except the contractors (as late as 1925 a Chinese was not allowed to stay overnight in Gallup). He talked of Manuelito, last war-chief of the southern Navahos; of "Old Dan" Dubois; of mountain men, traders, and trappers. Some of Cotton's stories seemed at the time to be a bit overdrawn, and it may be that they were shaped for my benefit, but others told of his active interest in civic affairs and of his efforts to improve Navaho craftmanship in both blanket-weaving and silverwork.

Improved silverwork and improved blankets increased sales, without question, but I judge Cotton's interest was essentially altruistic. While still at Ganado, so he said, he had imported Mexican silversmiths to teach their trade to the Navahos, and the latter naturally acquired a preference

107

for Mexican silver. Mexican coins were softer and easier to shape than those minted in Denver, and when Mexican coins were no longer available Cotton supplied bullion.

So, too, with blankets: he gave premiums for superior weaving and sought to enlarge his Eastern market with these blankets. His admitted error in this area, if I understood correctly, was his advocacy of aniline dyes as a substitute for native dyes. Aniline dyes speeded manufacture but cheapened quality and thus changed the whole blanket industry. In 1920, "Cozy" McSparron out at Chinle was striving to revive the native dyes, but he was only partially successful. Gathering the necessary plants and boiling them was too time-consuming even for a Navaho. Furthermore, the price-per-pound which traders were willing to pay was not considered adequate compensation for the extra work involved.

Although he had moved to Gallup in 1894, Cotton never forgot his old friends at Ganado. There were business connections to maintain. Also, he and Ed Hart drove out from time to time—the road was either sandy or muddy and ruts were always deep—just for a friendly game of poker with Don Lorenzo and the priest from St. Michael's. More than once, so he said, they poured out the holy water so that the bottle could be used as a candlestick. Subsequently, "perhaps about 1910," Cotton brought the first automobile to Gallup, "but I never dared tell my wife what it cost." That secret purchase was doubtless the spark that lighted Cotton's interest in highways and led, a decade later, to construction of the initial Route 66—graded here and there but axle deep in mud whenever it rained. He sponsored a road race from Gallup to Williams, Arizona, and another from Gallup to Albuquerque, 160 miles and seventeen hours distant. My co-workers and I drove that same road in 1920 and learned the adhesive properties of New Mexico mud at first hand.

108

There isn't much left of old Gallup today. The dusty streets of 1910 and even 1920 have been paved with macadam; electric lights line the curbs. An 1885 hotel and saloon at the east edge of town, later remodeled into an attractive, vine-covered cottage, was razed when Route 66 was widened. Remains of an old Butterfield relay station about fifteen miles to the south have gradually melted into the surrounding landscape. Exposed to summer rains and winter snows, adobe walls leave little trace.

East of Gallup are remnants of former tent towns—Coolidge, Thoreau, Guam, and Grants—that bloomed briefly as the Atlantic and Pacific Railroad plodded its way westward. Coolidge, so named for one of the railroad directors, had previously been known respectively as Bacon Springs and as Crane's Station, after "Uncle Billy" Crane, an army scout who served under Colonel Kit Carson. Lying in the shadow of the Continental Divide, Coolidge was famous during railroad-building days, so gossip has it, for the number of its saloons and the quantity of whisky they dispensed. Among its thirstiest customers were soldiers from Fort Wingate, ten miles to the west. All that is now left of Guam lies a mile east of Coolidge, and Grants lies thirty miles beyond at the edge of a lava flow.

When Mexico held title to this area and especially to that portion beyond the Zuñi Mountains, all was divided into vast land grants, and here sheep were raised by the thousand and owners grew rich. Out of this back country came a handsome young man one day, wearing a white sombrero, tight pants, and a gold-fringed jacket. He had the appearance of a wealthy sheepman and, indeed, claimed to be one. A few weeks later, however, after he had married the village belle and after his credit had run out, it became known that his acquaintance with sheep was only as a herder.

109

Edward Hart, the Gallup hardware merchant and a good friend of C. N. Cotton, had come over from England in the early eighties just at the end of the Lincoln County wars, to be a cowboy (a lithograph of Edward VII hung on the Hart kitchen wall in 1939). I never thought to ask what outfit he first worked for, but there were several large English and Scottish companies, including the L-C's and the Carlisles, operating in southern New Mexico at the time. Each employed Texans to ride herd and settle range disputes with sheep owners. Some of those Texans, Hart recalled, were inclined to be rough in their play, and when they started shooting at his feet to make him dance, he quit and followed the railroad west.

Spoofing the stranger has always been a popular pastime in the Southwest, and I have often been the victim. Also, when opportunity offered, participation seemed justified. Such an opportunity presented itself one summer when Dean Cummings had invited an Eastern professor to share his archaeological explorations in Arizona. We were working the Oljeto area and returned frequently to the trading post for supplies. Clyde Colville was too serious to participate in such nonsense, but John Wetherill was not beyond a little fun.

Because he was naturally quiet and retiring, John Wetherill has often been labeled taciturn and humorless. But quite the contrary. He was a Quaker to be sure, and not overly talkative, but he enjoyed a joke. I've seen him jest with his Navaho neighbors over the quality of blankets and hides they offered in trade or the amount of sand obviously added to increase the weight of their wool clip. And I've seen him join in more than one practical joke.

Perhaps the most famous of all practical jokes in which Wetherill participated was perpetrated at Oljeto in 1909 and had for its victim our visiting professor, not too trustful of

110

Indians and their ways. Navahos around Oljeto were still wild in 1909 and wore their hair long; two prospectors had been killed in Monument Valley a few years before, and their killers were still alive and living near by. These well-known facts offered an unparalleled opportunity.

Out among the canyons, after recurrent campfire conversations about the probability of open hostilities colored by recollections of surly-looking Indians met along the trail, came the night the Navahos "attacked" the Oljeto trading post and its occupants. Navaho bystanders loitering around the Wetherill home and its staked yard had watched the packing of duffle bags; they might have seen a nickel-plated revolver secreted in one of them. The visiting professor was leaving next morning, accompanying an itinerant minister through Monument Valley to Bluff City. The minister rode a white horse, but that had nothing to do with the journey or its destination.

Plans maturing during the day concerned only the professor and our solicitude for his well-being. To lessen the possibility of accident on the eve of departure, his nickel-plated revolver and ammunition were surreptitiously lifted from his saddlebag. Navahos watching through the fence looked mean; we must be on guard. With an attack imminent, it was thought that the professor could find maximum protection by secreting himself under a tarpaulin covering a rear-yard haystack and remain there until daybreak. But the professor was not so easily beguiled. He had greater faith in the security of the Wetherill kitchen and dashed for the open door at first hint of trouble and refused to leave. There was much shooting of firearms great and small about the house and corrals that night; much rasping of sticks along the stockade fence; much whispering among the defenders. Far-away night noises sounded like Indian signals. Dean Cum-

111

mings slept through the turmoil and arose bright and cheerful next morning to bid his guest and the missionary safe
journey, but those who actively protected the establishment,
including John Wetherill, were somewhat longer in recovering from the hazards of the night.

Next mail from Bluff brought a brief note from the professor: "Of all sad words of tongue or pen the saddest are
these: I'm stung again." The minister had returned the nickel-
plated revolver.

Playfulness was still popular in 1923 when the director
of the National Park Service, A. B. Cammerer, and I happened to be in Carlsbad, New Mexico, at the same time.
As we walked down the street together, three or four barefoot urchins in advance of us slipped up behind "Uncle Billy"
Washington, said to have been a member of Billy the Kid's
gang, and exploded a paper bag just to see the old man whirl
with a start at the rifle-like report.

I was in Carlsbad to appraise an "Indian skeleton" someone had seen in a deep cavern out west of town. My guide
for that adventure was a member of the state legislature and,
happily, he was known to everyone in Eddy County. This
good fortune was evidenced when we stopped one night at a
ranch back in the hills where strangers were seldom seen.
During our political visit there—every visit is a political visit
for a politician—we were shown a couple of near-by caves
where Billy the Kid had found refuge several times and where,
so our host told us, some of his companions had been buried.
Lincoln County was cow country in those days, and cattlemen and sheepmen kept a sharp eye on each other.

About 1880, as John Wetherill measured history one day
in Chaco Canyon, the Carlisle brothers and L-C's (sometimes called "the Lacys" and said to have been owned by a
Dr. Lacy) were running thousands of cattle on Indian land

112

between Hosta Butte, north of Thoreau, and the San Juan River. In 1907 both companies were securely entrenched on the public domain in the Monticello district of southeastern Utah, and I had dined at their tables. But Edward Hart, his cowboy ambitions behind him, had remained in New Mexico to watch the country grow and to treasure memories of the old days and such old-time friends as Don Lorenzo Hubbell, C. N. Cotton, and Dan Dubois.

"Old Dan" Dubois, a fabulous character, who spent part of his colorful life in the Gallup area, was one of the last mountain men—with incredible experiences about which he would say not a word. Harold Bell Wright and Zane Grey had each gone to Gallup with the express purpose of getting his story, and both went away defeated. Old Dan would not talk. Among his intimates mentioned herein were Lorenzo Hubbell, Edward Hart, Frederick W. Hodge, and C. N. Cotton. It was Cotton and Hodge who untangled enough of Dan's background to win for him admission to Sawtelle Soldiers' Home in Los Angeles, where he died on March 13, 1925, and was buried as Joseph Dubois.

Names and dates meant very little to Old Dan. He was born on a plantation in lower Louisiana about 1833, according to Hodge, his only biographer, and enlisted in the Union Army at Fort Cleveland, Ohio, on July 1, 1863, as Dennis Donovan, age nineteen. Previously in southern New Mexico or Arizona he had been captured by Apaches and had gone with them to Tiburon Island in the Gulf of California; later, in Upper California, he developed such a friendship for Joaquin Murieta, a notorious bandit of the 1850's, that he named a son after him. Since Dan would say nothing at all of his own past, his children and relatives supplied much of the data which Hodge recorded.

According to these informants and what Hodge, himself,

had gleaned during an acquaintance of nearly fifty years, Dan Dubois at various times had been a cowboy, a stagecoach driver, a dispatch rider between army posts in New Mexico and Arizona, an Indian trader, and an interpreter at Fort Defiance and elsewhere. He spoke Navaho and Spanish fluently; he could converse in Ute, Comanche, and French. He is reported to have married three of Manuelito's daughters and various others, Anglo, Mexican, and Indian. The Navahos called him "Iron Shirt" in recognition of his indestructibility, and those who knew said his broad body held a dozen arrowheads and at least seven bullets as evidence of disagreements along the trail. His rifle stock was inset with a mirror so that he could look backward as he rode to see who followed.

One of those enemy bullets, according to C. N. Cotton— and the story is repeated by Hodge—became troublesome after forty years and was extracted by a Mexican with a piece of baling wire at Dan's command. Old Dan had an abiding faith in baling wire as a surgical instrument, for he employed it in extracting his own teeth. He also had faith in the healing properties of whisky, good or bad, and used it generously as a preventive.

These and other tales of Dan Dubois were told to me in Gallup and along the trail. It was said that he had enlisted in California at the beginning of the Civil War as a Portuguese interpreter. Again, that he and another cowboy once rode up to Montana, with a few fights along the way, just to see the country. Since Hodge mentioned neither of these latter tales in his rare biography, they are probably to be regarded as just two more fabulous stories of a fabulous character.

On the only occasion I ever talked with Dan Dubois, in 1921, he was crippled by rheumatism and confined to a blanket-padded chair at his little trading post in Coyote Canyon, somewhere in the Zuñi Mountains southeast of Gallup. By Hodge's reckoning he was about eighty-eight at the time. Half a dozen mixed-blood children and grandchildren ministered to his wants, but the store shelves held nothing visible other than soda crackers and a few cans of axle grease. My two companions and I were seeking a protohistoric ruin which Dan was supposed to know about, but he had been without tobacco for several days and was in an ill temper. During the course of our conversation I gave him what cigars I carried and emptied my pouch at the end of our visit, but we left in a barrage of profanity and without knowledge of the ruin we sought. Two years later, at the dedication of the Fred Harvey Hotel, "El Navaho," on May 25, 1923, I saw Dan Dubois again when he shared the spotlight with several old Navaho warriors with whom he had exchanged rifle fire in younger days. The Indians looked upon Dan with amazement, but his admiration for them, if any, was silent.

"Old Dan" preferred the mountains in his later years and was seldom seen about Gallup. A more familiar figure there, one who met every train that passed El Navaho, was "Wild Dick" Hastings. Dick looked like a character from Death Valley but was not. He wore a mustache that out-mustached all others, a huge walrus of a mustache that thrust forward full from the upper lip and then swept away to either side with all the grace of a homing pigeon. It was a mustache without equal! Movie-makers tried to capitalize on it but realized that something more was needed. One day at Kayenta in 1917, Dick pushed back from the Wetherill table with a sigh of satisfaction and drew from an inner pocket a ten-inch black celluloid comb with which he proceeded to reorganize and caress his most envied possession. Never was there another such facial adornment.

Frederick Webb Hodge, a former co-worker of mine at the Smithsonian Institution, was excavating Hawikuh, one of Coronado's "Seven Cities of Cíbola," for the Museum of the American Indian, Heye Foundation, when I stopped off at his camp below Zuñi in 1920. As a trustee of the School of American Research he had participated in the 1910 summer session in Frijoles Canyon (of which more later), but his acquaintance with the Southwest began much earlier. He was a member of the famous Hemenway Expeditions, 1886–89, and then or subsequently came to know the historian George Parker Winship, famed Adolph Bandelier, Frank Hamilton Cushing, and others. Rugged Dan Dubois, whom we met at Gallup, was camp utility man for the 1888 expedition near Zuñi and had his full quota of adventures during the season.

While Hodge and I were standing together at Hawikuh, discussing a Spanish altarpiece that had been exhumed only moments before, our attention was drawn to a small group of Zuñi priests walking over from a summer farming community six miles away. The altarpiece had come to light less than ten minutes before; no one had left Hawikuh and, so far as we knew, no signal had been given by the Zuñi workmen. An unanswered question that still lingers with me is: How did those Zuñi priests know that a significant discovery had been made? There are those who do not believe in telepathy, but I am not one of them.

Partly in consequence of his editorship of the Bureau of American Ethnology publications, including the incomparable two-volume *Handbook of American Indians North of Mexico,* Hodge became a recognized authority on the aborigines of New Mexico and Arizona and of the Spanish colonial period. From the Smithsonian he moved to New York and the Museum of the American Indian, Heye Foundation; from there to the directorship of the Southwest Museum, Los Angeles. Fortunately, his lifetime notes and a voluminous correspondence have lately gone to the Southwest Museum for use of the students to follow.

Hodge was a delightful raconteur, and his field experiences when transportation was chiefly by four- and six-horse wagon provided endless innocent anecdotes—and some not so innocent. At breakfast in Holbrook one morning when he called for poached eggs, the waitress replied, "Sorry, sir, but our eggs won't poach."

A methodical individual and outwardly casual, Hodge never permitted the seriousness of the day to interfere with a practical joke. The hours which I spent at his Hawikuh camp were brightened materially when Dick, the expedition's Zuñi factotum, announced that there was something in his shoe and, to prove it, exposed his sockless foot and shook out the much-scuffed and mutilated body of a field mouse. No one ever knew how that dead mouse got into Dick's shoe.

In pre-air-conditioned days residents of western Arizona habitually countered summertime temperatures by sprinkling the upper sheet at bedtime and leaving the rest to evaporation. It was a common practice; everyone did it.

When I was pacing the station platform at Ashfork early one morning awaiting the Phoenix train, my attention was drawn to a shirt-sleeved man with long sunburned mustaches contentedly smoking a pipe while tipped back in his chair, his feet on the Fred Harvey railing. Just then two young ladies from back east emerged from the hotel lobby to sniff the morning air and complain about a hot, sleepless night. The smoker, without turning his head, audibly inquired, "Didn't you know enough to wet the bed?"

Although Mesa Verde National Park in southwestern Colorado was already well known to archaeologists and

117

others, having been established in 1906, it was not altogether accessible. The usual approach was from the east by way of the breath-taking, narrow-gauge railway between Alamosa and Durango or Mancos and thence by team. Anyone who would knowingly undertake the uncertainties of that ride really wanted to see the "green table."

However, 1920 brought an unexpected opportunity to reach Mesa Verde from the south, from Gallup on the Santa Fe. Three companions and I hired an auto and driver for the journey up and back; the announced distance of approximately 150 miles seemed within reason. But the dirt road which we were to travel was newly graded and without culverts; rain water and mud filled every ditch.

It was midafternoon when the five of us arrived at Cortez, "the pinto bean capital of the world," tired, dirty, and hungry. Mud-filled ditches and pushing had delayed us. We had had no lunch and suppertime was still three hours away. But the proprietress of the local restaurant took pity on us and volunteered to prepare a spot of tea. Her generosity was welcomed; we were all very tired, hungry and dirty.

When the tea arrived, knitted cozy on the pot and cups heated, it was as black as coffee. At first sip our driver made a wry face and exclaimed: "Mrs. Maple, that tea is too strong for me. Can I have some water?" To which Mrs. Maple replied: "I'm English, you know. When I make tea I make tea; and when I make water . . ."

Our approach to the crest of Mesa Verde next morning was up the old Point Lookout road, since replaced. It was a one-way road with no turnout. At the time of our visit it was controlled by telephone; from a box at either end one phoned ahead to make sure the way was clear. But once on top one was rewarded by superb distances and superb ruins: Cliff Palace, Spruce Tree House, Balcony House, and

118

others farther removed. J. W. Fewkes of the Bureau of American Ethnology was actively engaged with their excavation and restoration, but he did not see all that lay hidden among the cedars and piñons. After forty-three years I recently returned to the Mesa Verde to find new and improved roads everywhere, restful lodges for overnight guests, newly discovered ruins, and the remains of terraced gardens where pre-Columbian housewives had raised corn, beans, and pumpkins for their families.

Three years after that unforgettable trip I met my friends Kidder, Morris, and Sylvanus G. Morley in Gallup for a tight-scheduled trip to Pueblo Bonito, Aztec Ruin which Morris was then excavating for the American Museum of Natural History, Mesa Verde National Park, and back to meet a certain eastbound train at Gallup. Morley had brought as his guest from British Honduras a physician, Dr. T. W. F. Gann, under assurances that New Mexico aridity would prove a complete antidote for twenty years of tropical humidity. The four of us were to show Gann the archaeological high points of the Southwest in only three days.

But late summer 1923 proved to be the wettest in the recorded history of New Mexico. It rained from early August until mid-September. Never was there another such summer. We were caught in an after-season shower on our first day out. Rain began gently during a lunch-time stop in Satan's Pass, north of Thoreau. It rained all afternoon, increased in volume with distance from the railroad. Forty miles beyond and just as dusk was falling, we slithered through Chaco Canyon mud to shelter in my earth-covered kitchen, closed for the season and bulging with folded tents, cots, and excavation equipment. It rained all night, quietly and persistently.

At daybreak the ruins of Pueblo Bonito were awash and it was still raining. By unanimous consent, plans for the

119

local inspection were abandoned in favor of a dash for Aztec Ruin and Mesa Verde. But, from higher ground at the head of Mockingbird Canyon, the three branches of Escavada Wash were seen in full flood, and our party divided. Kidder and Morris with their companions continued north, taking all the dry wood in the second car; the rest of us turned back hopefully toward the Chaco. We carried rocks to fill mudholes, gathered all available brush for straightaway traction, pushed and pulled, and finally abandoned our car and dragged wet bedrolls through the last muddy half-mile. We were too exhausted to prepare supper. The ordinarily dry Chaco Wash was a raging torrent; escape was impossible; it would be days before we could cross successfully.

Because he had arranged to meet the eastbound California Limited two days later, Morley was understandably annoyed with the situation in which we found ourselves. The Chaco arroyo was in flood; it was anyone's guess when one could cross to the south bank in safety—perhaps in one week, perhaps two. At the end of the first day, I arranged with a Navaho for two saddle horses, and a third for suitcases, to be ready at daybreak next morning. The man and his horses arrived on schedule, but the equipment was makeshift—one saddle without stirrups; one horse without a bridle. For five dollars the Indian was to deliver Morley and Gann at the Crownpoint Agency, thirty miles distant, in time to catch the mail stage to Gallup. And then confusion began.

Morley's horse, following close behind the guide's, was across the flood and up the slippery dugway while Dr. Gann lingered to photograph the crossing. When he mounted to join Morley, pocketing his camera meanwhile, the unguided horse naturally took the shortest possible route toward those on the opposite bank. But the bank was steep and slippery;

120

the unshod horse slipped backward into quicksand, Gann slid off the rear end and waded back to us, while the Navaho, his mind on that five-dollar fee and the sun mounting higher, took off at a gallop with Morley racing to keep up.

The Crownpoint short cut stretched across open country, uphill and down. There was no stop along the way, not even an Indian hut. Morley's knowledge of the Navaho language was limited to one word, *chineago* (food), and this he used repeatedly as a brake, so we later learned, to slow his guide to a more comfortable pace.

Under pressure for time the Navaho had begun his day on an empty stomach, while his charge was fortified with a partial breakfast and a luncheon of cold baking-powder biscuits garnished with strips of cold bacon. When Morley reached what he considered the limit of physical endurance, he would call out *"chineago."* The Navaho would stop and take the proffered biscuit without comment and then start off again at the gallop.

There is more to the story, but it need not be told. That thirty-mile cross-country ride was a continuing torture. Looped ropes in lieu of stirrups put friendship to the test. Morley arrived at Fred Harvey's Gallup hotel that same evening, but he could not sit down. At the announced moment next morning he boarded the Limited, transacted the business in hand, and stepped down again at Albuquerque.

Left friendless and alone in New Mexico, Dr. Gann spent two miserable days with me in Chaco Canyon. The rain had slacked momentarily, but high water still raced down the arroyo. Our underground camp kitchen was crowded with stored equipment, leaving no space for exercise. The valley floor was a lake of mud and every step strained thigh and shank. With no place to go, the hours dragged. Finally, his low shoes scarred and misshapen, our deserted guest was put aboard another eastbound train. He never returned to the dry, desert-like climate of the Southwest.

Despite mud in the rainy season and sandstorms at other times, Chaco Canyon remains a favorite refuge of mine. It was there that I directed a seven-summer research program for the National Geographic Society (1921–27)—a program that centered about Pueblo Bonito but included such related subjects as dendrochronology, sedimentation, and soil analysis. The famous old ruin covers more than three acres in ground area, and four distinct types of masonry are represented in its three hundred rooms; razed walls and village debris lie twelve feet beneath the surface. But all of this has previously been described and illustrated in publications of the Smithsonian Institution, the National Geographic Society, and other scientific bodies.

The National Geographic Society's researches at Pueblo Bonito were inaugurated in 1921 and continued on schedule until their conclusion in 1927. We did our banking and much of our shopping in Gallup both because it was then, as now, the principal town in west-central New Mexico and, if the truth must be told, because the Fred Harvey hotel, El Navaho, offered a hot bath and a good night's rest on every trip to town.

On our way to and from Gallup we passed Thoreau ("Threw," in local pronunciation) at the mouth of Satan's Pass, gateway to the former Indian agency at Crownpoint. An important construction center while the railway was building, Thoreau had withered perceptibly since 1882; only three saloons survived in the early 1920's when I bought groceries there. Leading merchant at the time was B. I. Staples (C. N. Cotton said the initials stood for "Big Indian . . . he knows more about the Indians than they know about

122

themselves"), who had arrived from New England on a stretcher a few years previously and somehow had found his way to renewed health and the red cliffs of Thoreau. In 1920 he and Mrs. Staples lived across the road from the store in a dirt-roofed house walled by railroad ties on end, but five years later he had built a sprawling sandstone home astraddle the Continental Divide a mile to the west.

At this new location which he named in honor of a fellow New Englander, Calvin Coolidge, Staples built a "trading post" and workrooms for craftsmen and thus created a tourist attraction that gradually evolved into a retreat for artists, writers, and archaeologists. Prehistoric ruins underlay his front yard. The largest Navaho rug that I had ever seen occupied the living-room floor. To encourage an increase in the quality of handmade Navaho blankets and silverware, a business ambition probably influenced by his friend Cotton, Bert Staples increased the prices which he paid for superior products and took samples east for private exhibit. Then, as has happened elsewhere, highway engineers relocated Route 66 and left Staples' new establishment high and dry, with the red sandstone cliffs of Thoreau at his back.

When we frequented it, between 1921 and 1927, Thoreau was seventy miles from Chaco Canyon—if weather favored. During the rainy season I always sent two cars out together for weekly provisions. At such times the drivers carried their bedrolls and were prepared for an overnight camp. By preference Chaco Canyon is now approached from the north, and the road that we traveled from Thoreau eventually will be replaced, so they say, by a black-top connecting Routes 66 and 44. A macadam road even now climbs through Satan's Pass, replacing the rocky stream bed which, from sheer necessity, we had to follow.

It may have been during our second summer in the Canyon

that half a dozen Navaho dogs from a hogan beside the road found amusement racing our cars and biting at the front tires. To teach a neck-twisting lesson my drivers tied bulging burlap bags over the hubs, but, on their first trip thereafter, the dogs never wakened and the bags were still in place when the two cars pulled up to the loading platform in front of Staples' adobe store. Coincidentally, a big black limousine with Eastern tags arrived at the same moment, and the lady in the rear seat leaned out to ask why the hubcaps were covered. B. I. Staples, thoroughly Westernized after only three years' local residence, answered quickly: Satan Pass, through which the cars had just made their way, was so narrow that hub protection was necessary.

A couple of years later, in the middle twenties, I happened to be present when a carful of Okies stopped at Staples' for gas. And I have never forgotten the picture they made: a man and his wife, both weather worn from long days on a wind-scoured Oklahoma farm, with four or five children and grandma in an old Model T with beds and bedding roped to the top, spare tires hanging from both sides, a galvanized iron tub tied on behind, and a goat fenced on one running board. They were all tired from tiresome miles on the road and uncertain about the future. My companions and I loaded our purchases and turned north toward Chaco Canyon, but memory of that weary family, buoyed by visions of a brighter tomorrow, lingered with me for years and, indeed, still lingers.

Chaco Canyon is mentioned again both because it was my home, summer after summer, and because some of the men mentioned herein were met along the trail to and from the canyon. Among others, there was Jack Martin, a former freighter for the Hyde Expeditions and my sometime teamster; and there was Joe Lovelady, a lonely cowboy at Smith's ranch who married a mail-order bride from Kansas City and regretted the choice almost immediately. The bride arrived on schedule, equipped with red hair and all else that seemed necessary, but when she saw her future home, a one-room board shack overlooking the watering troughs and the corrals, she insisted upon instant return to Thoreau and a through ticket back to K. C. Joe belatedly realized that his own cooking was all he needed anyway and that a bride would be no help in repairing barbed-wire fences and cleaning water pockets.

Jack Martin was considerably under six feet tall but as bowlegged as the traditional Texan. He had driven cattle up the long trail to Abilene but had turned to freighting "when they started to fence in the whole country." In his younger days, said Jack, Texas miles were measured by wire fences: "You got up at daybreak and rode all day and when you came to a fence, that was a mile."

In 1920, Martin's pride was a team of magnificent bays. They pulled his wagon, water barrels at each side, on my reconnaissance of the Chaco country. We visited each of the great Chaco ruins and decided which to study intensively. On a second trip for review of my conclusions, Jack and I were accompanied by three long-time friends whom I greatly admired and whose advice I always valued: A. V. Kidder, Sylvanus G. Morley, and Earl H. Morris. Morley had won his spurs among the ancient Mayas of Guatemala and lower Mexico; Kidder and Morris were our foremost authorities on the prehistoric Pueblo peoples of the Southwest and their ancestors, the Basket Makers. Diverse stories, some disparaging and some true, grew out of that exploration-by-wagon, but it was a memorable trip, scarcity of water and edibles notwithstanding.

During the initial phase of our reconnaissance, Jack Martin and I stopped several times to water our horses at the old Richard Wetherill well—a dug well with windmill in the arroyo at the Chaco crossing. Both windmill and well were washed out by floods a year later, but what water could be drawn by rope and bucket was under the watchful eye of Ed Doonan, a barrel-chested Irishman employed by Edward Sargent of Chama, New Mexico. Wetherill was killed by a Navaho in 1910; thereafter his local properties were leased by Mr. Sargent, who ran several flocks of sheep in and bordering Chaco Canyon, and his Mexican herders were supplied by Doonan. Doonan, in turn, had been wounded by a night-prowling Navaho a year or two before we arrived, and he held a strong antipathy to all members of the tribe. So far as I could observe, his days were spent mostly in the sunshine on his doorstep, guarded by a large anti-Navaho dog.

The buildings which Doonan occupied at the southeast corner of Pueblo del Arroyo, a large rectangular room with smaller rooms adjoining, were built in 1898 for purposes of the Hyde Exploring Expeditions. Known successively as "the hotel" and "the store," those rooms, I would guess, originally served as a boardinghouse for Expedition employees, balancing a former bunkhouse outside the northeast corner of Pueblo del Arroyo, that they later became "the hotel" to house and feed the increasing number of Expedition guests. When the place was renamed "the store" I cannot surmise, unless Doonan sold miscellaneous supplies there between 1910 and 1918 while working for Sargent. Thereafter, Sargent's Mexican herders needed little more than beans and coffee. Gus Griffin tried a small store there in the middle 1920's, but it was short-lived.

Richard Wetherill's famous trading post, hub of the far-flung Hyde Expedition empire, likewise was built in 1898, abutting the west end of his residence at the southwest corner of Pueblo Bonito. Residence and store and all other Wetherill

126

buildings except "the hotel" have since been razed by the
National Park Service in connection with its development
of Chaco Canyon National Monument. The Hyde Exploring
Expeditions came to an end about 1905, but the rutted roads
traveled by its freight wagons still survive for those who know
where to look.

Some time in 1921, after Sargent had taken his sheep elsewhere, an itinerant minister came by and settled into the
quarters which Doonan had vacated. He was a broad-shoul-
dered, middle-aged man, rather severe of countenance and
not much given to conversation. His first act, once adjusted
to his surroundings, was to sweep the large rectangular room
and erect a temporary lectern facing a succession of wooden
benches. Next he posted a three- by five-inch notice on a
porch post (the porch has since been removed) announcing
Sunday-afternoon services at 3:30. Local Navahos could not
read and, anyway, they had planned to spend that particular
Sunday afternoon breaking horses to ride. They had a grand
time both in and out of the round corral which Wetherill had
built on the arroyo bank but missed the 3:30 service, and
so did I. The minister left early Monday morning without
farewells and not very hopeful, I fear, for salvation of the
people whom he left in Chaco Canyon.

Another unanticipated visitor that same summer, 1921,
was the owner or lessee of two six-horse wagons that came
down canyon late one afternoon, turned around in our door-
yard, and left without a word. Those wagons were piled high
with bedrolls and other gear; water barrels and buckets hung
at each side; three or four saddled horses followed behind.
There was a vast assortment of equipment in those two
wagons, but we never learned whether it represented a prospective Indian trader seeking a new location or a party of
Easterners looking for experience on the wild frontier. We

127

saw absolutely no one other than the two drivers, and they simply turned around and headed back up canyon without so much as a wave of the hand. We never learned where they came from or where they went.

Six-horse freight wagons were seen more frequently in eastern New Mexico at that time, usually from Mexican sheep ranches and sometimes with oxen substituting for horses as they hauled huge brown bags of wool to the railroad. Nowadays, of course, every Mexican sheepman has his own five-ton truck.

Pueblo Bonito, the focus of our studies in Chaco Canyon, was first described in 1877 by W. H. Jackson, famous photographer of the Hayden Surveys. Jackson was a photographer by profession, and after the Civil War he photographed Plains Indians in Nebraska and the Dakotas; thereafter, he photographed the building of the Union Pacific Railroad, and, beginning in 1870, he photographed the scenic wealth of the entire Rocky Mountain area for F. V. Hayden. During those years Jackson's negatives were made on glass and were processed in a portable darkroom of his own devising. But in 1877 he tried a new product, films, and unfortunately lost what otherwise would have been the first photographic record of the great Chaco Canyon ruins.

A decade after Jackson, Victor Mindeleff of the Smithsonian Institution surveyed and rephotographed those same ruins in connection with his incomparable study of Pueblo Indian architecture. Although Mindeleff and I later came to know each other in Washington, D.C., and there compared mutual experiences, we never worked together in the field. Victor Mindeleff will always remain to me a man of artistic temperament who had known western trails from horseback.

One even closer than Jackson and Mindeleff to my studies in Chaco Canyon was A. E. Douglass. In 1921, when we first met, he was director of Steward Observatory at the University of Arizona and an astronomer of international note. One of his specialties was the effect of sunspots upon vegetation, and in his search for evidence he had developed a method of reading the age of western forest trees from their annual growth rings. It was this that brought our paths together, for I reasoned that if growth rings could tell the age of a forest tree, they could also tell the age of timbers used in Spanish colonial buildings and from there back into pre-Spanish times. It was simply a question of reading backward from the present into the unrecorded past.

Between 1922, when Douglass began his analysis of wood from Pueblo Bonito, and 1929, when he finally ascertained the approximate age of the great ruin, the National Geographic Society sent three expeditions into the field in search of older and older house beams. The color of pottery from prehistoric ruins became a clue that narrowed the search, and here, because of their knowledge of such pottery, Harold S. Colton, director of the Museum of Northern Arizona, and two of his assistants, Lyndon L. Hargrave and Emil W. Haury, contributed materially to the success of our effort to determine the age of Pueblo Bonito.

Colton, a zoologist from classrooms in the University of Pennsylvania, had become interested in local archaeology while summering near Flagstaff. From that natural beginning he had extended his researches until he had to build both a laboratory in which to study his collections and a museum in which to house them. In 1929, when he and I worked together on the dating problem, Colton had appropriated space in the Women's Club building, and that, as it happened, was the first step toward the present Museum of Northern Arizona.

Once firmly settled at Pueblo Bonito in 1921, we began

129

the annual practice of inviting certain co-workers in other disciplines to spend two or three days in camp with us in consultation on matters of mutual interest. Douglass, the "tree-ring man," and those closely associated with Indian life and agriculture, north and south, were among the first participants invited. Our idea seemed such a good one that it was repeated in 1923 and 1925. But we found that distance from the railroad and the limitations of our facilities were too great. Then, in 1927, Kidder inaugurated his famous Pecos Conference, and we were content to end ours.

The age of Pueblo Bonito having been determined, we turned next to the geologic history of Chaco Canyon. For this task Professor Kirk Bryan of Harvard, the Geological Survey's authority on sedimentation and ground-water resources of the Southwest, was a happy choice. Unlike New England–born Douglass, Bryan was a product of New Mexico. He knew the land and its people. He could speak Mexican like a native, and he could eat chili con carne with either hand. During the two summers he spent with us in Chaco Canyon he traced the course of a prehistoric arroyo past Pueblo Bonito and found in the valley fill artifacts representing two distinct civilizations: the first and more primitive, from the lower sixteen feet; those of a higher culture, from the upper strata. Among these upper-strata people were the builders of Pueblo Bonito.

Wind- and water-deposited alluvium raised a question about productivity, and here I had the co-operation of C. S. Scofield, a soil chemist and, at the time, in charge of the U. S. Department of Agriculture's Office of Western Irrigation Agriculture. Soil samples from the upper nine feet of that Chaco alluvium showed such an excessive amount of sodium salts, or black alkali, that, in the opinion of Scofield and his staff, aboriginal agriculture would have become increasingly unproductive. Together, black alkali and Bryan's prehistoric arroyo could have caused abandonment of Chaco Canyon by its prehistoric farmers.

During occupancy of Pueblo Bonito the inhabitants were primarily concerned with getting enough to eat. But some among them were artists of no mean ability. From the older portion of the village remarkable ceremonial paraphernalia were collected, and from four contemporary burial rooms the National Geographic Society retrieved hand-painted baskets, bone and stone finger rings, pendants made from Gulf of California shells, and ornaments of sky-blue New Mexico turquoise. Among the last none attracted more attention than the four-strand necklace, with its two pairs of matched ear-bobs, now exhibited in the Hall of the Explorers, National Geographic Society building, Washington, D.C. There are approximately 2,500 graduated beads in that necklace, each individually selected for color and individually shaped for its place in the chain. The owner of that necklace must have been a very outstanding member of the community.

Equally newsworthy, however, is the excitement which this priceless ornament caused at time of discovery. Within seconds, almost every Indian on the job—both Zuñi and Navaho—was there, leaning over the fragile masonry of the old house, intent upon clearing operations at floor level, twelve or fourteen feet below. They knew intuitively that something unusual had been found. This unheralded assembly reminded me of the time five years earlier when I had watched several Zuñi priests approach Hawikuh from their summer colony six miles away to see the historically significant specimen which had been unearthed minutes before. It was another case of Indian intuition or mental telepathy!

Colored photographs of that incomparable necklace and its paired earrings stirred envy in the manager of Fred

131

Harvey's Indian curio shop in the Alvarado Hotel at Albuquerque. Twice each summer, going out to Pueblo Bonito and returning, I would stop off to see what new treasures he had acquired. Always there was something to make me envious in turn: a Chilkat blanket from the Northwest Coast or a trophy from the head-hunters of Ecuador. On one such visit he brought from his vaults a turquoise necklace "the equal of yours from Chaco Canyon." But the individual beads undeniably represented small lots from many different ruins, brought together on one string for display and sale to some imprudent collector.

Recently, while visiting in Santa Fe, my wife and I were luncheon guests of the Honorable Daniel T. Kelly at Fred Harvey's La Fonda. The waitress seemed vaguely familiar, and when our host remarked that she had started with the Fred Harvey company in Albuquerque forty years before, I innocently inquired if she perchance had known the former manager of the museum. "Did I know him," she exclaimed, rushing from one table to the next. "Would you believe it, I was still new on the job and a stranger in town when he invited me up to his room for a drink. I didn't drink anything but sarsaparilla at that time, but two weeks later when he repeated the invitation, I accepted. We had a quiet drink and then another. And would you believe it, nothing happened."

George M. McLellan, the only cook who worked for me at Pueblo Bonito more than one season, had cooked for loggers, miners, and railroad crews as well as for archaeologists. He stayed with us three successive summers, and I shall never cease to be grateful. Camp-cooking was his profession, but he was more than a professional cook. He was a most agreeable companion. An omnivorous reader, he counted among his prized possessions an arm-long shelf of

132

five-cent paperbacks—a history of the world and all human knowledge. From his reading Mac could describe such wonders as the catacombs of Rome, the pyramids of Egypt, or the art galleries of London and Paris in minute detail and with the appreciation of a connoisseur. He was at home in any company. When his own day's work was done, he came to share ours at the ruin. A bachelor by preference, and a frugal one, Mac lost his lifetime savings with the collapse of a California banking syndicate and retired shortly thereafter. He was a wonderful man to have around camp, and he shamed us all for the little we had learned in college.

Another equally dependable member of my Chaco Canyon staff was O. C. "Pete" Havens. Pete came to us from B. I. Staples' store at Thoreau as a stenographer and bookkeeper. But soon thereafter he was doing everything that needed doing. He was that rare individual in an archaeological camp—a "man-of-all-trades." He could take an auto engine apart and put it together again without the loss of a single nut; he kept our gasoline pump going to supply the daily ration of water for Mac's kitchen and for wall repairs at the ruin. In addition, he drove out once a week for mail and supplies, and he took most of the pictures that illustrated my several archaeological reports. Hence it was a great personal pleasure for me when Pete and his son, another ardent photographer, were free to join Mrs. Judd and me in the summer of 1966 for a return to the spectacular Betatakin Ruin, Monument Valley, and Rainbow Bridge.

George Halla, or Hallisha, became my handyman at Pueblo Bonito. He called himself "Georgie Washingtone" and applauded his own erudition. He arrived from Zuñi with the first load of workmen, but when it soon became apparent that our pick-and-shovel job in the ruin was too strenuous for one of his years, he was elevated to the position of camp

133

tender. I explained his responsibilities: filling the water pitcher in each tent every morning, sweeping out the sand if necessary, fetching wood or coal for the cook, and other small chores. George would nod his head to each explanation and say, knowingly, "O.K."

Also there was the matter of potsherds from the excavations. These had to be washed and dried and, above all, each lot must be kept together. We were gathering statistics concerning type and quantity, hence the importance of room or trench numbers. George and I talked a patois of our own —a mixture of Zuñi, Mexican, and Navaho; and when my vocabulary failed, which it did frequently, I added a little English. But, whatever my instruction, Halla always nodded with complete understanding and his inevitable "O.K." Not until our third season did I learn that "O.K." was the only English he knew.

"Black Bottom" so named from a popular 1927 song, was a Navaho toddler who liked Mac's cookies and spent a generous portion of each day at our camp waiting for more. His father was one of my workmen; his mother, a former schoolgirl, had converted a dugout beside the arroyo crossing into a makeshift home. Understandably proud of her only son, she took maternal pride in creating for him assorted necklaces of copper bells, wooden beads, and spools but left his rear side entirely unadorned.

During my seven summers for the National Geographic Society in Chaco Canyon, it was our practice to have a Sunday-night bonfire out in front of the expedition tents while our Zuñi workmen entertained themselves and the rest of us with impromptu songs and dances. Only the scarcity of firewood limited the entertainment to a single night. Navaho neighbors rode in from their homes and sat on their horses

at the edge of the firelight, seemingly enjoying the perform-
ance as much as we.

On one such Sunday we had as our guest a British general
from India, touring the Southwest in pith helmet and jodh-
purs. Repeatedly during the evening he voiced surprise that
we dared to expose ourselves before a campfire. He had
served long on the frontier of India, where it was practically
suicide to be silhouetted by a light of any sort. He was delighted with our impromptu entertainment and interested in
our impassive Navaho audience, but he simply could not
understand that our Indians differed from his Indians.

On weekday nights individual Zuñis often sang for their
own pleasure to the accompaniment of a cottonwood-and-
horsehide drum. The cottonwood came from a dead tree; the
horsehide, from a Navaho pony that did not watch where it
was going and fell into one of our exploratory trenches. We at
camp had become accustomed to these after-dark concerts
and paid no attention to them. But one morning, just at flag-
raising time, a frightened tourist appeared suddenly and
exclaimed, almost tearfully: "Thank God for sight of the
American flag once more and a white man." When he had
gained control of himself, I learned that he and his family,
motoring out the unmarked road to see Pueblo Bonito, got
stuck in the sand a mile up canyon and could go no further.
The night being pitch dark, he could see absolutely nothing
and did not know where he was; hearing the drum and the
wild, unfamiliar singing, he had feared that he was in hostile
territory.

Among regular Navaho guests for our Sunday-night bon-
fires were Dan Cly, one of my Navaho excavating crew, his
mother, a sister, and the latter's daughter. All except the
daughter were undersized, but I lacked the wit to make

135

thorough inquiry while opportunity offered. The old mother was a Zuñi by birth, and it was said that she had been stolen or captured by a Navaho when about fifteen. Unfortunately, I did not seek the truth of this statement. She was known throughout the Chaco country as "the Zuñi woman." She remembered a few Zuñi words and some of the more prominent tribesmen of her youth. She conversed with my Zuñi workmen in a mixture of Zuñi and Navaho but refused their invitation to return home. Her home, she said, was among the Navahos; her husband and her children were Navahos; she had lived among them all her life. Dan, the son, was of small stature like his mother and so was his sister, Jessie. But Jessie's daughter was a big, strapping Navaho like her father. Two of Dan's younger sisters, so I was told later, had returned to Zuñi and married there.

It was in the fall of 1922, I believe, that Frederick V. Coville, chairman of the National Geographic Society's Committee on Research, was finally persuaded to make an on-the-spot investigation of our Chaco Canyon field work. To my infinite delight he brought with him those well-known world travelers, Gilbert H. Grosvenor, president of the Society, and Mrs. Grosvenor. All three were well bundled against the cold autumn winds, but they gained a lasting impression of the haunting beauty of the canyon and the magnitude of the Society's undertaking.

In later years when I was lecturing in Washington and elsewhere, Mr. Grosvenor, from the wealth of his experience, gave me a bit of advice that paid huge dividends. "Always," he said, "outline the breadth of your lecture in the first few moments and never, never hold an audience more than an hour and a quarter."

Motoring along an open road one day, I met a charming Navaho grandmother, en route for an indefinite visit with

136

neighbors. She was alone but thoroughly self-reliant. Even her family refused to worry over her independence: "She'll be back when peaches are ripe."

Without conscious selection on my part, many of the Zuñi men whom I took to Chaco Canyon were members of the Macaw clan. They told me that, within memory of their elders, there had never been a live macaw in their village. Such feathers as they periodically needed for prayer offerings were purchased from Santo Domingo pueblo, over near Albuquerque. Knowing all this, I decided to give them a macaw of their own but took particular pains to tell the Sun Priest that the gift was for all the Macaw people although I was leaving it with him, as their leader, for safekeeping.

When I next saw the bird fifteen years later, it was still alive but clearly had been called upon for too many sacrifices. Not long thereafter I received at Washington a telegram from the Sun Priest: "The parrot is dead. What are you going to do about it?"

In 1959, I returned to Chaco Canyon for dedication of the National Park Service's new Visitors' Center with its well-conceived and informative local museum. But my thoughts at the time were focused less upon construction and exhibits than upon the more conspicuous changes of thirty-odd years. During my studies at Pueblo Bonito, 1921–27, we drew our drinking water from a dug well in the arroyo. A sheet-iron box covered with burlap and dampened by a dripping pan on top seemed to us the last word in refrigeration. Gas lanterns furnished our light. Now they have electricity in Chaco Canyon—and refrigerators, and deep-freeze units, and water flowing freely from nickel-plated faucets, and telephones (albeit with thirty-seven parties on the line), and flush toilets replacing our old two-hole standard.

Also, they now have a bridge across Chaco Wash—a god-

137

send not fully appreciated, I fear, by Park Service personnel. Before it was built in 1928, every passing flood meant for us repair work at the crossing. Both banks were too steep and too slippery when wet. And always, within twenty-four hours after a cloudburst, came a tall, thin man on his way to Farmington for baled hay. He was a home-grown mechanic as evidenced by his truck. It had once been a Model T, but the rear seat had been removed and a broad, flat deck substituted. Riding free on the deck was his "toolbox," approximately three feet square and a foot deep, half-filled with rusted horseshoes, bolts, washers, and nuts. That man was just psychologically unable to leave an unattended scrap of iron beside the road! There were no floor boards under his steering wheel; none was needed since his feet were always busy with the pedals. A two-foot length of faded red inner-tubing replaced a lost radiator cap.

One day we were all on the job regrading the north approach to the crossing—teams, men, and supervisors—when this unknown freighter made a dash through flowing water, his red radiator tube swaying and spouting steam, and got halfway up the north incline before his engine coughed and began to falter. He called to a boy behind: "Give me that wrench in the toolbox." The boy handed him a thirty-inch Stillson with which he reached down and administered an authoritative whack to the engine housing; then he was off, up over the top of the dugway, and on into the distance.

Later that same summer, or perhaps the following year, our hay-hauler met a competitor hub-deep in the sand two miles east of our camp. He stopped to offer help, a custom of the period, and stayed for supper. During the evening the two men fell to boasting of their respective vehicles. One had an engine beyond compare but the chassis was weak. The other was reversely handicapped; his truck was sturdy enough to haul anything, but the engine could not pull it except when empty. Conversation continued well into the night and was resumed over breakfast coffee. Within two days a trade had been effected. They traded engines. Despite the fact that one engine was a trifle narrower, a little bending of the other's frame provided a satisfactory adjustment and both men resumed their accustomed vocations, freighting from Thoreau to Farmington and back again.

To return to an earlier time, in 1910, after three summers as a student archaeologist with Professor Byron Cummings, I was invited by the director of the School of American Research, Edgar L. Hewett, to join him for field work in New Mexico. Our season began and ended in Santa Fe.

Excavation of Tyuoni ruin, in Frijoles Canyon forty-odd miles northwest of the city, was to be our principal undertaking, but first came the annual summer session (the second) of the School and its Board of Trustees. Physical comfort for individual members of the board was a matter of prime consideration. Tents and cots were arranged under the cottonwoods, and an open area beside the stream was reserved for meetings. To avoid a commissary, the Director had arranged with Judge and Mrs. Abbott, who maintained a summer home in the canyon, to provide meals for the entire company. And when it came to foodstuffs the Director drove a hard bargain. The three pancakes which we workingmen were allowed at the Abbott breakfast table were undeniably the thinnest pancakes ever served in New Mexico. I was one of the supervisors but was handed a shovel upon arrival.

El Rito de los Frijoles ("Little Canyon of the Beans") has since been absorbed by Bandelier National Monument, but it had a name of its own in 1910. There was then no smooth macadam highway to the canyon floor, no local museum and

139

restaurant to welcome and refresh the visitor. The old road was devious and unforgettable. Only those who really wanted to go ever went to Frijoles Canyon.

From Santa Fe we traveled by narrow-gauge railroad, locally known as "the chili line," to an abandoned lumber camp, Buckman, and there transferred to a two-horse wagon to cross the Río Grande on what remained of a corduroy road and so up to the crest of Puyé Mesa. If most of us walked the distance, it was because the old logging road followed a dry stream-bed, rough and rocky, and the wagon had no springs.

Like Buckman, "the chili line" has been uprooted and all but forgotten since 1910. Previously it had carried freight and occasional passengers to Alamosa, in southern Colorado, and way stations along the line. According to Santa Fe gossip this narrow-gauge railroad had been built at a fixed cost per mile, hence the lack of bridges and the roundabout way in which the rails avoided every gully and barranca. It had all the deviousness of the narrow-gauge line between Alamosa and Durango but lacked the picturesqueness of the latter run.

From the Frijoles overlook, two hundred feet above stream level, all our supplies—foodstuffs, bedrolls, and tools—had to be manhandled down a gravelly path to the canyon floor. Anticipating the pick-and-shovel work to follow, Don Beauregard, the artist, and I had taken refuge in a suite of six connecting rooms carved in the tufa cliff high above the campsite. Dwelling places carved into the tufa cliffs form one of the main features of Frijoles Canyon. Terraced houses were built out in front, on top of the talus and against the cliff. Upper rooms in those houses—second, third, and fourth stories—connected with rear rooms carved from the granular rock, and they undoubtedly proved very satisfactory to the original

140

builders. By setting up residence in six of them, Don and I thought to escape daily meetings and evening lectures at the main camp.

Our seclusion was short lived, however; it lasted only until Charles F. Lummis and his guitar arrived from Los Angeles. As one of the trustees, Lummis was entitled to the very best the camp offered, so he moved into a couple of caves just around the corner from ours, lit one of his big black Mexican cigars, and made himself at home.

A former newspaperman and a correspondent for the *Los Angeles Times* during the Geronimo campaign in the middle eighties, Lummis had twice walked across the continent and had written half a dozen books reporting his adventures. He was the founder and first director of the Southwest Museum at Los Angeles and a recognized historian of the Spanish colonial period. He wore no hat to cover his silken white hair but affected a broad Mexican sash by way of a belt. An intimate friend of Theodore Roosevelt, Lummis was the only man, I am reasonably sure, who ever attended a White House reception in a brown corduroy suit, a Mexican sash, and Navaho moccasins.

More to the point, Lummis was one of those who believed, along with Edison and Steinmetz, that no man needed more than three hours' sleep. So he sat beside a small fire outside his cave and entertained members of the summer session with old Spanish and cowboy songs until 3:00 A.M. He knew every cowboy and Spanish song ever written but only one set of chords for the guitar. Despite the rather steep climb up from camp everyone came to hear those songs, and they were worth hearing. But what Lummis and the others overlooked on these nightly concerts was that we assistants, unlike trustees, worked from 7:00 in the morning until 5:00 at night.

Edgar L. Hewett, director of the School of American Re-

141

search, then and now a branch of the Archaeological Institute of America, was, as I said, in charge of both the 1910 summer session and the Tyuoni excavations. From the presidency of the Las Vegas Normal School his interest in archaeology led, successively, to various ambitious undertakings: excavating among ancient Maya ruins in Guatemala, a Museum of Man at San Diego, and summer classwork for university students in Mexico, Peru, and elsewhere. Where I knew him, in Utah (1907 and 1908), in New Mexico (1910), and in Guatemala (1914), he made his supervisory inspections in noticeably short time and then took off for another field. A master salesman, Hewett probably did more than any other individual to check the exploitation of prehistoric ruins in Colorado, New Mexico, and Arizona. He, above all others, saved the great ruins of Chaco Canyon. But he was never the outstanding archaeologist he was thought to be. There are those who will protest this personal opinion —but I base it upon my knowledge of him in various places and under variable conditions.

We had good company in Frijoles Canyon that summer of 1910 even after the Board of Trustees had come and gone. Professors Junius Henderson and Wilfred W. Robbins of the University of Colorado were there gathering geologic and botanical data for a joint publication. Miss Maud Woy, of Denver, and Miss Barbara Friere-Marreco, of London, were studying ethnology. F. W. Hodge, of the Smithsonian Institution, and Sylvanus G. Morley, later to become famous as a Maya scholar with the Carnegie Institution of Washington, were resting briefly from the burdens of office. And there were Chapman, Harrington, Nusbaum, and Adams from the regular staff of the School in Santa Fe.

Our working crew consisted of Tewa Indians from the pueblos of Santa Clara and San Ildefonso. When the Director announced one morning that J. P. Harrington wanted to learn their language, there was a surplus of Tewa volunteers. But they didn't know Harrington. He was a master linguist and absolutely relentless in pursuit of a new word or a new interpretation for one heard before. After a couple of days he was able to converse with them in their own language and trapped his informants repeatedly in giving false information.

Years later Harrington and I were long associated at the Smithsonian, he with his languages and I with my archaeological laboratory. Search for unrecorded or forgotten languages took him from Alaska to Patagonia and back again and on around the world. At merest hint of a last survivor at some remote native village, he was off like a hawk in pursuit of a sparrow. His chief fault, if it is a fault, was his readiness to drop a subject once he had satisfied his curiosity. Things commonplace to most men were new and novel to Harrington. And his forgetfulness led to inconvenience that would have embarrassed anyone else. At least once, to my knowledge, he returned by bus from the depths of Mexico with railroad fare in his pocket.

Upon conclusion of excavations in Tyuoni several of us were sent to examine prehistoric remains along the Río Chama and its tributaries. Old Santiago Naranjo, then governor of Santa Clara pueblo, accompanied us as cook and general factotum, his long gray hair bundled at each ear and wrapped with strips of beaver fur. Where he acquired that fur I never learned, but it served him well for many years.

Our first camp was made under a cottonwood near the onetime health resort of Ojo Caliente, its hot mineral springs still flowing but the rambling frame buildings evidencing neglect and disrepair. Whatever its past glory, Ojo Caliente offered very little to guests in 1910. Our preference was for open camp under the cottonwoods.

143

A half-mile or so up the valley, a large pre-Spanish ruin of crude masonry had largely collapsed upon itself. I have forgotten the queer Tewa name by which it was known at the time. We were to clear a few rooms and learn what we could in a fortnight. Every morning, just as we arrived to begin the day's digging, a gray-bearded Mexican appeared from a near-by house to work along with us. He never said a word, but he watched closely what we were doing. He may have thought we were looking for gold—the usual charge against archaeologists—but since he confined his own efforts to tracing the exterior of the building, we let him alone. He used a short-handled shovel but moved a lot of earth.

The old gentleman made progress with his self-imposed task until one of the students, noting that our co-worker never brought lunch, offered him a cold baking-powder biscuit thickly spread with peanut butter. Unused to such fare our fellow explorer took one generous bite and then, choking and blowing, rolled downhill to the irrigation ditch, thrust his face in full depth, and drank deeply. That was his last day on the job. He never spoke to us again.

From Ojo Caliente we journeyed farther north and there, surrounded by small Mexican-American settlements, set about copying pictographs etched on the surface of basalt boulders. The hills were literally carpeted with those boulders—thousands of them—each carved with a figure unintelligible to us but perhaps meaningful to the carver. We copied hundreds of those pictographs and then set forth on our return to Santa Fe. What we did not know, however, was that passengers on "the chili line" had an obligation in operating the one train per day.

Every little settlement along the way—nameless or otherwise—was provided with a trackside loading platform but no station. By burro-drawn conveyance our bedrolls and

144

camp equipment were hauled to the nearest such platform; the driver was paid and took his leave with an airy *"Hasta la vista."* There were no other passengers and no one to tell us we had to flag the train to a stop.

Eventually the train whistle sounded in the distance. We all came alert and made mental check of our individual luggage. As the three-car train came hurtling down upon us we stood there, shoulder to shoulder, like a reception committee at a fair, but there was no reduction of speed. As the engine approached we edged forward in group anticipation, ready to climb aboard. Our signs were unfamiliar to the train crew and moments too late. As the engine rocked past, a head bellowed from the cab window: "Why the hell didn't you wave?"

Before we could reply, the baggageman called from his open door: "Why the hell didn't you wave?" The engineer was applying the brakes, but momentum was too great and the train rolled on down the track. As it did the conductor, with a firm grasp on the handrail, leaned forward from the rear platform to demand: "Why the hell didn't you wave?"

Because we had not known the local custom, our train had to come to a full stop and then back up to the platform on which we were standing. Our equipment was hurriedly loaded and then we, too, climbed aboard for the last few homeward miles. Santa Fe's "chili line," justly famous in its prime, has since gone the way of all living things and left a great void.

145

VII

CASTING MONUMENTS IN GUATEMALA

THREE YEARS after I went to Washington, Edgar L. Hewett asked the National Museum to lend my services to supervise the reproduction of certain Maya monuments at Quiriguá, Guatemala. The reproductions were to be featured in the proposed Hall of Man at the Pacific-California International Exposition in San Diego. In correspondence I had recommended the use of glue molds rather than the papier-mâché squeezes then in vogue, but glue had never been tried in the humid tropics and its efficacy was doubtful.

After I had consulted with New England pattern-makers on the problems anticipated, the necessary materials were purchased and shipped in the autumn of 1914—among other items, six barrels of plaster of Paris and one barrel of plasticine. However, the customs official at Puerto Barrios knew nothing of plasticine and refused to release the barrel without instructions from Guatemala City.

While awaiting these instructions—and it is possible that they have not yet arrived—we improvised with ordinary jungle mud. Earl H. Morris was excavating a near-by temple and Sylvanus G. Morley was copying and translating its inscriptions for the School of American Research, while Wesley Bradfield, Ralph Linton, and I concentrated upon making replicas of the stone monuments selected by Director Hewett.

Quiriguá is part of an ancient Maya religious center of temples, commemorative monuments, and stelae situated on

146

the northwest side of the Motagua River fifty-odd miles from the Gulf of Honduras. In 1910, when the United Fruit Company began development of its vast banana plantations in this area, it set aside as a national reservation a seventy-five-acre tract embracing this part of the ancient center. A remnant of the original forest encloses the park—giant ceibas and mahoganies a hundred feet high and a variety of palms —in which macaws, parrots, and other tropical birds were constantly flying and squawking from one lofty perch to another. At Quiriguá station, on the Puerto Barrios–Guatemala City railroad, the Fruit Company maintains, or formerly maintained, an excellent hospital for its personnel and a hotel for passers-by. There were fifty-one insects, as I recall, that bit and laid eggs in warm-blooded animals, man included, and all bit us sooner or later.

With scant concern for Morley and Morris and their respective tasks, Bradfield, Linton, and I turned to our own responsibility, that of casting in plaster the indicated monuments. After a little experimenting, we were ready to begin. We soon discovered that the rich valley mud, freed from coarser vegetal matter, made a satisfactory substitute for our lost plasticine. Banana ribs substituted for sturdier wood; banana fiber, for hemp.

It was our practice first of all to scrape off the lichens and then thoroughly scrub that portion of the monument to be cast. A two-inch layer of mud was spread directly upon the carved stone and then a layer of reinforced plaster upon the mud. Fibers from dead banana stalks, of which there was an inexhaustible supply close at hand, replaced the Manila rope which we lacked for strengthening the plaster shell. Sections of this shell, of a length and width convenient for handling, had to be braced and closely fitted at the ends.

Every afternoon the plaster shell and its underlying layer

147

of mud were removed, and the carved stone was thoroughly scrubbed again. The mud went into a galvanized iron tub for re-use while the plaster forms were reassembled in proper order, braced and bound together with plaster-soaked fiber to guard against expansion. Then we were ready for the melted glue that would replace the mud layer and provide a negative imprint of the carving, faithfully reproducing its every surface irregularity.

Our working crew, selected with the advice of the local Fruit Company manager, were intelligent, resourceful men. A majority were Jamaican Negroes. They quickly learned our procedure, and work progressed smoothly despite resentment at repeated use of the scrubbing brush. Galvanized iron tubs formed a double boiler for melting the glue; there was mahogany in abundance for fuel and banana fiber for reinforcement. Because several thousand acres of United Fruit Company bananas surrounded us, it was a simple matter to have two or more stems of the fruit ripening in our work shed at all times. This practice promptly gave substance to a local company fiction: "Only natives and archaeologists eat bananas." After all, bananas were sold by the pound up in the States; here they could be had for the taking. And we took them, several dollars' worth at a time.

With a portion of the monument freshly scrubbed and clean, our plaster shell was returned to position and its several sections firmly tied together with more plaster-soaked fiber. Then the melted glue was poured in, replacing the mud, and left to harden overnight. Next, in the maximum coolness of predawn, the form and its glue lining were taken down again and a plaster positive quickly made from each section of the glue negative. This was the uncertain phase of our operation, since setting plaster generates a good deal of heat and we had no ice to cool the glue.

148

In due time these plaster positives, properly assembled and painted to approximate the stone monuments which they reproduced, were installed in the Hall of Man at the San Diego museum. They remain there today, a fitting tribute to the genius of the ancient Maya priesthood.

Because of its proximity to our respective assignments, we northerners elected to share the two-story house of the local division manager rather than stay at the Fruit Company hotel several miles away. A gasoline motorcar made short distance of the intervening miles when it ran, but sometimes the engine balked and sometimes the branch line was blocked by a train of banana cars on the way to Puerto Barrios. Most important, however, was the fact that our glue negatives had to be peeled during the coolest moments of the day. We just could not bother with a railroad motorcar.

Our host, the manager, was a short, rotund gentleman with an edgy temper and a pronounced Louisiana accent. He habitually wore white linen riding breeches and leather puttees, with a gun forever on his hip. His orders, we noted, received prompt attention. He may or may not have been married—we never inquired—but he kept a native mistress parked with the caretaker's family over at the ruin. A Negro man did his cooking; a Guatemaltecan youth, the remaining housework. Because of his obvious command of the local situation and his generous physique, our host was promptly dubbed "the Padre."

Something of a ballooning effect seemed to follow the Padre, walking or riding. One could not miss his white shirt and his breadth of white breeches. His days were largely spent on the plantation (twenty thousand acres, if I recall correctly), riding its narrow trails to supervise his cutters and the quantity of fruit that they harvested. Jamaican Negroes did the responsible work such as lowering the

149

banana stems and then felling the empty stalk with one stroke of the machete.

Being new to all this, I was interested to note that a single jab of a knife on the end of a twenty-foot pole half-severed the stem on which the fruit grew, and that weight alone carried the bunch down to the shoulder of the "catcher," generally a native Guatemaltecan, who loaded it on a mule for transportation to the nearest branch-line receiving station. The Fruit Company had its own private railroad which picked up these piles of bananas and hauled them to the main line at Quiriguá station and thence to a company boat at Puerto Barrios. Word of the boat's expected arrival was, of course, known in advance so there would be no waiting about for fruit-laden cars.

The Padre's two-story house rested upon concrete pillars four feet high. All domestic water drained off the galvanized roof where buzzards roosted, and a daily chore of the house-boy was to see that the water was strained and thoroughly boiled. Since the young man, with other matters in mind, was inclined to be forgetful at times, our host often emphasized previous instructions with a couple of well-placed shots near bare feet. The cook, a sandaled Jamaican with a gold ring in each ear, was more reliable, and, additionally, he was an excellent cook. I have an enduring memory of the dishes he contrived with black beans and bananas.

In 1914 all work stopped in Guatemala during Easter week. Irrespective of religion, no one worked. Since there was nothing we could do about it, the five of us set out for Guatemala City to see the cathedrals, the art galleries, the museums, and the religious processions. From Quiriguá station the railroad generally followed the Motagua River upstream, and the scenes on either side were strange to most of us. Women, with small children playing about, were doing the family laundry at river's edge, pounding white garments on water-worn boulders, seemingly oblivious to large and small alligators dozing not far away.

We had lunch at Zacapa—a delicious fresh-fruit salad of avocados, mangoes, and papayas sprinkled with maguey worms, toasted and powdered. Lunch was accompanied by a fruit drink that called for repetition. But here and at every other settlement along the line, vendors of tamales, enchiladas, and tortilla-wrapped rice crowded close to hawk their wares to hands outstretched from car windows. The traveling Guatemaltecan is always hungry! At least twice during the morning our engineer slowed down in passing clusters of palm-thatched huts to give opportunity for a squad of soldiers led by an officer with upraised saber to dash out in search of fresh army personnel. Irrespective of age, only those fleet-footed men who reached the security of the jungle escaped the recruiting party.

We arrived in Guatemala City a day too late. All activity had come to an end—even the ubiquitous horse-drawn cabs —and we had to walk to the Grand Hotel. From this center, operated by an enormous Jamaican Negro, we walked to the city park, justly famed for its magnificent relief map of the Republic; we walked to the national museum especially to examine certain archaeological treasures of which we had heard. We walked to various other public buildings and found all closed. It was Easter week. Where we wanted to go we walked. There were no cabs. Even the horse-drawn trolley cars were idle—open-sided cars pulled by a horse at the end of a long chain, a chain just long enough, we surmised, to let the driver apply his brake before bumping the horse.

Only the numerous churches were open for inspection and for the processions that all day long wound their toil-

151

some way from one church to another. We spent several hours with the American consul watching from his balcony some of these processions—casually crowded men, women, and children clustered about half a dozen or more sandaled or barefooted carriers straining under the weight of an enthroned Biblical figure decorated with ribbons and paper streamers, mirrors, and artificial flowers. It was a day for the Indians primarily, and salvation came to all who participated. The city elite, some with mantillas and high shell combs, had made their obeisance earlier and in private.

At week's end we returned to our unfinished tasks at Quiriguá and found the Padre in a dither. Ordinarily, disputes among his workmen did not especially trouble him, but this time a Saturday-night brawl at the far end of his jurisdiction had resulted in a killing. I rode out with him to make his inspection. It was a brutal and bloody mess. There had been too much pulque consumed, and the argument had been settled with machetes. In consequence there was not enough left of one disputant to warrant an official report. Native funerals in Guatemala can be simple and brief.

In due course it was time to box our plaster casts and take our departure. We were all delighted to learn that the Padre would be sailing with us; after all, we had come to know him in his own home, and there was a degree of satisfaction in prolonging the acquaintance aboard ship. Whether he was returning to the States on vacation or to seek another job we never knew. He was a self-appointed individual, and wherever he went he took command. He did not like the German coffee-grower from upcountry who shared our table and told him so; he called him a "squarehead." The German pressed fingers to his head, front to back and sidewise: "It ist not skvare. You can see dot."

After leaving Belize, capital of British Honduras, we ran

into rough weather. The sky turned mean and the waves rose higher, but the Padre did not miss a meal. He was a rugged sailor on sea or land and he liked good food. On our last morning out of New Orleans, with the ship rolling and plunging, only the strong appeared for breakfast. The Padre lengthened his arm and surveyed the menu. "Waiter," he commanded with finality, "bring me an order of tripe with brown gravy." The waiter turned toward the galley but was called back. "Just double that order."

On the Fruit Company wharf at New Orleans we said our several farewells and went our several ways. And the Padre quietly walked out of our lives.

In this final paragraph I wish once more to emphasize the fact that I never considered myself one to point the way. The trails which I followed between 1907 and 1930 were mostly well marked, but traveling has since been made easier. Air mattresses and sleeping bags have replaced sweaty saddle blankets. Pack mules and pack saddles have virtually disappeared. Folding gas stoves have replaced the Dutch oven; the tin pot and Arbuckle's coffee are relics of yesterday. During field work as a student of archaeology—nine expeditions for the Bureau of American Ethnology, five for the Smithsonian Institution, ten for the National Geographic Society—I met many helpful men and some who were less so. Most of my thirty-nine years at the National Museum were spent among the exhibits or in the archaeological laboratory, classifying and recording collections newly received or those not adequately cared for at time of receipt. In retrospect, those thirty-nine years were productive and rewarding.

153

INDEX

Abraham, Utah: 70
Adugigei gorge, Utah: 30 ff.
Alamosa, Colo.: 118, 140
Albuquerque, N.M.: 108, 121, 132, 137
Alfred Vincent Kidder Award: 17; *see also* Alfred Vincent Kidder
Alkali Ridge, Utah: 21 ff.
Allen, "Aunt Jane": 15
Alpenstock, Frederick Wilhelm: 55–56
American Anthropological Association: 17
American Museum of Natural History: 119
Anasazis: 16, 31, 87
Aneth, Utah: 26, 27
Antelope Valley, Utah: 66, 67, 80
Antiquities, American: *see* U.S. National Museum
Apache Indians: 84, 113
Archaeological Institute of America, The: 4, 17, 141–42
Archaeology: 23; as a profession, 23–24; doctorate schooling available in, 54–55; of Greece, 54; of Mexico, 55; *see also* excavations, U.S. National Museum
Architecture: *see* excavations
Arizona: 29, 64, 94, 95, 104, 110 ff., 142; exploration of, 26, 73–86; importance of irrigation in, 82
Arizona, University of: 4, 83, 129; State Museum at, 4
Armstrong, Utah: 10
Armstrong Canyon, Utah: 9, 13
Artifacts: 130; *see also* excavations, U.S. National Museum
Arts and Industries Building, Smithsonian Institution: 47
Ashfork, Ariz.: 117
Atlantic and Pacific Railroad: 106 ff.
Augusta Bridge, the, Utah: 7 ff; *see*

also Natural Bridges National Monument, "The Presidents," Sipapu, White Canyon
Aztec Ruin, N.M.: 119, 120

Bacon Springs, N.M.: *see* Coolidge, N.M.
Balcony House, Colo.: 118
Bandelier, Adolph: 116
Bandelier National Monument, N.M.: 139
Basket Makers: 30, 98, 125
"Bear Cave Ruin, The," Utah: 12
Bear Springs, N.M.: *see* Fort Wingate, N.M.
Beauregard, Don: 42, 140–41
Beaver, Utah: 63, 64, 69
Beaver Creek: 79; *see also* Wall Creek
Beliza, British Honduras: 152
Benjamin, Marcus: 46
Benow, Chief Johnny: 20
Betatakin Ruin, Utah: 36–37, 42, 44, 76, 95, 101 ff., 133; restoration of, 86–94
Billy the Kid: 112
"Black Bottom" (Navaho child): 134
Black Mesa, Utah: 30
Black Mountain, Ariz.: 28
Black Rock Desert, Utah: 70
Blanding, Utah: 9
Blue Mountains, Utah: 7, 19, 76
Bluff City, Utah: 5 ff., 14 ff., 25 ff., 32, 33, 40 ff., 64, 76, 101, 111, 112
Boas, Franz: 55
Bobzien, Edwin: 82
Boies, L. C.: 83, 84
Bosque Redondo, N.M.: 38, 42, 94, 106
Bradfield, Wesley: 146, 147
Bradley, Lee: 102
Bright Angel Creek: 79, 80

155

160

Steinmetz, Charles P.: 141
Steward Observatory: 129
Stockwell, R. A.: 82, 83

Taft, William Howard: 17
Tater Canyon: 74
Terry, Charles T., Jr.: 52
Tewa, Ariz.: 104
Tewa Indians: 142, 144
Third Mesa, Ariz.: 103
Thompson, A. H.: 79
Thompson's Spring, Utah: 5ff., 19
Thoreau, N.M.: 109, 113, 119, 122ff., 133, 139
Tiburón Island, Gulf of California: 113
Toroweap Valley, Ariz.: 81
Tsegi Canyon, Utah: see Segi Canyon, Utah
Tuba City, Ariz.: 85ff., 94, 102
Tyende Creek, Ariz.: 37
Tyuoni ruin, N.M.: 142, 143

United Fruit Co.: 147ff.
United States: 70–71, 89, 148, 152
U.S. Army: battles Navaho Indians, 38–39; makes aerial survey of Pima Indian Reservation, 82
U.S. Department of the Interior: 37, 85, 88, 95
U.S. Exploring Expedition: 58–59
U.S. Geological Survey: 54, 62, 79, 100, 130
U.S. National Museum: 18, 21, 45–60, 66, 98, 99, 146, 153; see also Smithsonian Institution
University Museum (of Utah): 3
Utah: 113, 142; explorations of, 3–18, 19–26, 30–45, 61–81, 86–101; see also excavations
Utah, University of: 3, 4, 32, 50, 63, 86
Utah Indians: 71
Utah Lake: 62
Utah State Museum: 31
Ute Indians: 16, 17, 20, 39, 43, 68, 86, 98, 99, 114

Verdure, Utah: 7
Vermilion Cliffs: 77

Walcott, Charles D.: 46, 78–79

Walhalla Plateau: 79
Wall Creek: 79–80; see also Beaver Creek
Washington, D.C.: 17, 21, 28, 46ff., 53ff., 61, 73, 84, 85, 90, 91, 98, 128, 131, 136, 137, 142, 146
Washington, "Uncle Billy": 112
"Washingtone, Georgie": see George Halla
Water-Supply Paper 380: 100
Weston, Jack: 74, 75
Wetherill, Ben: 36
Wetherill, Betty: 101, 102
Wetherill, Fanny: 101, 102
Wetherill, Ida: 36
Wetherill, John: 25ff., 86ff., 93, 95–101, 102, 106, 110ff., 127; befriends Navaho Indians, 26–30; explores Utah, 34–45
Wetherill, Louisa: 32ff., 40, 43, 45, 102; Hoskininni claims her as granddaughter, 38ff.
Wetherill, Richard: 35, 125ff.
Wetherill In Motel, Utah: 102
White Canyon, Utah: 26, 32, 41, 98; exploration of, 3–18; natural bridges at, 7ff., 32, 33; naming of, 8, 17; monument to, 17; see also Augusta Bridge, Carolyn Bridge, Edwin Bridge
White Mesa, Utah: 7
Wilkes, Charles: 59
Willard, Utah: 61
Williams, Ariz.: 80, 108
Wilson, Woodrow: 27
Winship, George Parker: 116
Works Progress Administration: 59–60
Woy, Maud: 142
Wright, Harold Bell: 113
Wyoming: exploration of, 60–61

Yellow Rock Spring, Ariz.: see Pipe Spring National Monument
Young, Brigham: 50, 64, 78

Zion Canyon, Utah: 80
Zion National Park, Utah: 65
Zuñi Indians: 79, 116, 131, 134ff.
Zuñi Mountains, N.M.: 109, 115
Zuñi, N.M.: 116, 133, 136
Zuñi Sun Priest: 137
"Zuñi woman, the": 136